ANTIQUE PORCELAIN

John Sandon

Meissen candelabrum, c.1755

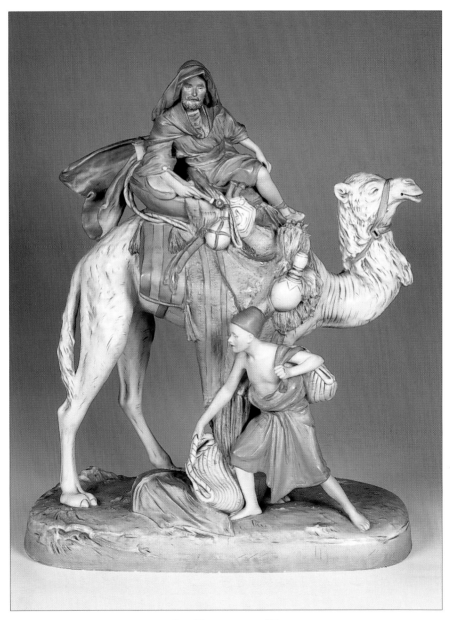

Royal Dux – see page 110

STARTING TO COLLECT SERIES

ANTIQUE PORCELAIN

John Sandon

ANTIQUE COLLECTORS' CLUB

ISBN 1 85149 242 9

British Library Cataloguing-in-Publication Data
A catalogue record for this book is available from the British Library

*The author and publishers acknowledge the help of Phillips,
International Fine Art Auctioneers, who have provided most of the
illustrations for this book, either photographed specially or drawn
from their extensive archives.*

Printed in England
by the Antique Collectors' Club Ltd., Woodbridge, Suffolk
on Consort Royal Era Satin paper
supplied by the Donside Paper Company, Aberdeen, Scotland

The Antique Collectors' Club

The Antique Collectors' Club was formed in 1966 and quickly grew to a five figure membership spread throughout the world. It publishes the only independently run monthly antiques magazine, *Antique Collecting*, which caters for those collectors who are interested in widening their knowledge of antiques, both by greater awareness of quality and by discussion of the factors which influence the price that is likely to be asked. The Antique Collectors' Club pioneered the provision of information on prices for collectors and the magazine still leads in the provision of detailed articles on a variety of subjects.

It was in response to the enormous demand for information on 'what to pay' that the price guide series was introduced in 1968 with the first edition of *The Price Guide to Antique Furniture* (completely revised 1978 and 1989), a book which broke new ground by illustrating the more common types of antique furniture, the sort that collectors could buy in shops and at auctions rather than the rare museum pieces which had previously been used (and still to a large extent are used) to make up the limited amount of illustrations in books published by commercial publishers. Many other price guides have followed, all copiously illustrated, and greatly appreciated by collectors for the valuable information they contain, quite apart from prices. The Price Guide Series heralded the publication of many standard works of reference on art and antiques. *The Dictionary of British Art* (now in six volumes), *The Pictorial Dictionary of British 19th Century Furniture Design, Oak Furniture* and *Early English Clocks* were followed by many deeply researched reference works such as *The Directory of Gold and Silversmiths,* providing new information. Many of these books are now accepted as the standard work of reference on their subject.

The Antique Collectors' Club has widened its list to include books on gardens and architecture. All the Club's publications are available through bookshops world wide and a full catalogue of all these titles is available free of charge from the addresses below.

Club membership, open to all collectors, costs little. Members receive free of charge *Antique Collecting*, the Club's magazine (published ten times a year), which contains well-illustrated articles dealing with the practical aspects of collecting not normally dealt with by magazines. Prices, features of value, investment potential, fakes and forgeries are all given prominence in the magazine.

Among other facilities available to members are private buying and selling facilities and the opportunity to meet other collectors at their local antique collectors' clubs. There are over eighty in Britain and more than a dozen overseas. Members may also buy the Club's publications at special pre-publication prices.

As its motto implies, the Club is an organisation designed to help collectors get the most out of their hobby: it is informal and friendly and gives enormous enjoyment to all concerned.

For Collectors — By Collectors — About Collecting

ANTIQUE COLLECTORS' CLUB
5 Church Street, Woodbridge Suffolk IP12 1DS, UK
Tel: 01394 385501 Fax: 01394 384434
———— or ————
Market Street Industrial Park, Wappingers' Falls, NY 12590, USA
Tel: 914 297 0003 Fax: 914 297 0068

Contents

Chapter 10. GERMANY cont.

Chapter 11. ENGLAND cont.

Introduction

Pottery… 'made as fine as glass drinking cups, the sparkle of water can be seen through it…' So wrote a ninth century traveller of Cantonese porcelain. From its earliest days porcelain has mystified and delighted kings, princes and noblemen. Collections were formed in palaces, castles and stately homes as oriental porcelain earned fortunes for successful traders. Once priceless and almost unobtainable, since the eighteenth century porcelain has become plentiful. Functional sets are used in every home while ornaments adorn mantelpieces and china cabinets around the world.

Collecting porcelain can become a compulsive disease, but it is a joyous affliction nobody ever regrets. Its very vulnerability is a major strength, as collectors cherish the rarity of pieces which have survived without damage for maybe two hundred years and still retain the subtle beauty or eccentric flamboyance which they exhibited when they were made and first went on sale in the china shops of the past. Today they grace antique shops, fairs and auctions and modern day collectors can pit their wits against the knowledge of the antiques trade, always on the lookout for a bargain. This book offers practical advice which enables even beginners to enjoy the hunt and capture of beautiful pieces of porcelain.

This is a very personal view of a subject I love. I have written a detailed introduction to all of the principal factories where porcelain was made. My facts have been checked using the standard reference works and I have acknowledged this help by listing these books at the end of each factory heading. I have received other assistance and photographs from Desmond Healey and Keith Baker of Phillips' Oriental and Twentieth Century departments; Peter Oosthuizen, a specialist in Dutch ceramics; and Letitia Roberts of Sotheby's in New York who has allowed me to illustrate American porcelain she has sold. My rather individual use of grammar was corrected by my wife Kris who provided much support during the writing of this book, as did my dear friend Michael Poulson who tragically died just as the project was nearing completion. His practical advice and ability to look at my text from an impartial viewpoint helped me to write for the beginner as well as the specialist, and Michael's own enthusiasm will be greatly missed.

Many of the illustrations were taken specially for this book by Chris Halton. Others are my own work as, with Chris's help, my personal photographic skills have developed. In the great majority of cases, where no individual acknowledgement is given, all illustrations show pieces sold by Phillips. This book would not have been possible without access to the precious archive of pieces which have passed through my hands during twenty-two years as a specialist at 101 New Bond Street, London W1. I now direct Phillips' International porcelain department and handle some of the world's most valuable specimens. At the same time my work with the BBC Antiques Roadshow brings me into contact with humble and mundane chinaware owned and loved by ordinary people. I enjoy walking round a car boot sale just as much as a specialist ceramics fair, and because of this I can advise beginners as well as dedicated collectors with years of experience. All are welcome to consult me at Phillips, for there is nothing I like more than to share my love of porcelain with fellow enthusiasts. I wrote this book with this in mind and I can ask for nothing better than the knowledge that my inspiration is helping new collectors to develop their own love for the beauty of porcelain.

John Sandon

CHAPTER 1

Advice to Porcelain Collectors

Collecting a popular shape such as these 'Nodders' becomes compulsive and it is important to keep an eye on value. For the price of these rare examples (including Meissen and Minton) it would be possible to buy six times as many ordinary examples in German bisque. The expensive examples are likely to prove a better investment.

I cannot advocate too many hard and fast rules, as collecting has to be a personal thing. All collectors have their own views on what is right for them, but the two governing factors are always the same – how much money can you spend and how knowledgeable are you? Collecting habits have to be adapted to meet these criteria. It is no use setting your sights way above your pocket, and to collect wisely you have to know what you are doing. It is important to seek the right advice and not to be afraid to ask for guidance.

All sorts of things start people off collecting – a chance inheritance, a lucky find, memories from childhood perhaps. Before you get carried away, you need to decide right from the start what sort of collector you want to be. 'I just buy what I like' is so often heard, and this is a great sentiment. The danger of a totally open approach, though, is a general collection that is nothing more than a hodgepodge. Without a theme, any collection misses out on

a great opportunity. Most collectors begin as generalists, testing the ground and discovering what it is about antiques that attracts them. It doesn't take long to realise that you are more interested in one kind of thing than any other. At a general antiques fair, what type of stall do you linger at? What kind of objects do you enjoy most on the BBC Antiques Roadshow? Without realising it, you are becoming a specialist. The degree of specialisation depends mostly on the knowledge available to you. There is nothing wrong in pursuing rarities, but if what you seek is too obscure it will be hard to find friendly dealers and other collectors to share your interests. You also need to decide early on if you want to go for quality or quantity. It goes without saying that unless you have unlimited funds you can't have both.

I have valued and sold many fine porcelain collections over the years, and also many extensive but disappointing ones. I offered once a collection of nearly two hundred teapots

If a piece of porcelain is rare enough, such as this Ming moon vase from the reign of Yongle, it will still be valuable when broken. With a damaged top this sold for £34,500 in December 1995.

that had been formed by a collector on a typically limited budget. She had paid £5 to £10 each to begin with and after fifteen years of rising prices she had been paying £100 or so. The result was two hundred very ordinary teapots. The few rarities were in poor condition or had been totally chance finds. If instead of buying fifteen teapots each year she had bought only four or five, she would have amassed about seventy nice examples for the same investment. It can be argued that collecting in this way would not have been such fun, but the choice of quality is a decision that needs to be made early on. I well remember when I was starting out in antiques, Geoffrey Godden told me and other collectors that we should all buy the best that we could afford. Everyone scurried to buy the interesting odd cups and saucers and damaged pieces that he always had on sale at his study weekends, but far fewer bought his more costly specialist

pieces in fine condition. I took his advice and dug deeper into my pocket to buy better pieces, and have never regretted this. The good items have given so much more pleasure and have increased in value many times more than the bits and pieces I could have bought.

If you haven't got a lot of spare cash you can still collect wisely. The secret is to choose a category that is generally less expensive, so that you can buy fine examples within your price range. Do not try to collect early Meissen as all you will be able to get are poor examples, rubbed, damaged or ordinary. Instead choose Chinese Export plates or Art Deco and 'Fifties teawares or Victorian jugs, just to take a very few examples, where you can still buy some of the best examples for under £100. Whichever less expensive category you choose, you must try to stick with it so that it grows into something meaningful.

Many of the beautiful items illustrated in this book are in good condition and frightfully expensive, so what about buying damaged examples. The age-old questions must always be asked. Can you live with a damaged piece? —Some collectors can, others simply cannot stand owning anything other than perfection. Does the price reflect the damage? Unless an item is incredibly rare, a broken piece should cost far less than a perfect one. Is it stable? Will that gaping crack get worse? What is under that ancient overpainting? Perhaps the most important questions of all are – could I easily re-sell it and how easy is it to get a better example when I want to upgrade? If an item is relatively common, then you will find it very hard to sell again if it is damaged. Basically, don't buy damaged specimens of common items. On the other hand I greatly enjoy owning some very rare objects that I could never have afforded if they had not been smashed to bits. In their way they give me a great deal of pleasure.

Upgrading is a vital part of a successful collection. It is necessary as your knowledge increases and when you find you want to buy better pieces. One major problem is having to part with well-loved pieces you bought when you were starting out. You naturally become attached to them, but it is important to keep

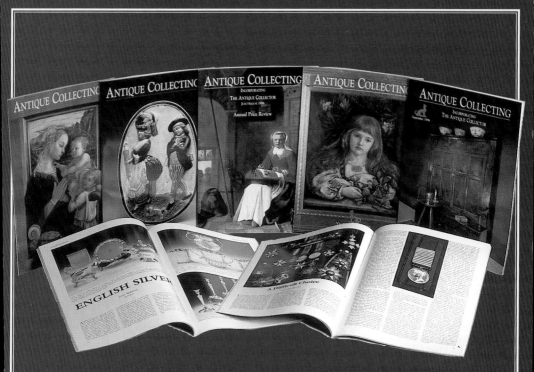

ANTIQUE
COLLECTING

FOR COLLECTORS • BY COLLECTORS • ABOUT COLLECTING

BOOKS

* Antique Collectors' Club publish authoritative reference books on antiques and the fine and decorative arts. Subject areas include art reference jewellery, gold and silver, metalwork, furniture, ceramics, glass, horology, textiles and collectables. Since 1968 over 400 titles have been published and many of these are now regarded as the standard work on their subject area. They are used extensively by collectors, appraisers, antique dealers, museums auction houses and galleries.

* In addition Antique Collectors' Club publish books on architecture and gardening, some of which appear under the imprint Garden Art Press.

A full colour catalogue of forthcoming and back list tiles is available free of charge on request from either the UK or US offices.

ANTIQUE COLLECTING MAGAZINE

* A year's subscription to ANTIQUE COLLECTING brings you ten issues of a full-colour magazine carrying a unique blend of authoritative articles from leading experts in antiques, art and collecting, in-depth practical information and exceptional illustration. Issue by issue it builds into an invaluable source of reference that you will read, keep and refer to again and again.

* Every issue of ANTIQUE COLLECTING carries features on a wide range of realistically affordable items and includes guides to their value, as well as regular news of saleroom prices, calendars of auctions and fairs, selected advertising and reviews of new books.

* Furthermore, all subscribers to the magazine enjoy privileged access to the publications of the Antique Collectors' Club. You will have the opportunity to buy new titles at significant discounts before they are available to the general public, as well as receiving exclusive offers and advance information throughout the year.

Why not join them and discover the benefits?

- - - ✂ -

ORDER FORM

☐ Please send me *Antique Collecting* magazine
(10 issues per year) @ £19.50 UK/ £25.00 overseas/ $40.00 USA/ $50.00 CAN
I enclose a cheque payable to: **Antique Collectors' Club** or
please debit my VISA/MC/AMEX card

Card no. .... Expiry Date ....

Signature...

Name..

Address..

.... Post/Zip code ....

Daytime Telephone Number...

I am interested in *Antique Collecting* magazine and would like to receive a free sample copy ☐

ANTIQUE COLLECTORS' CLUB, 5 CHURCH STREET, WOODBRIDGE, SUFFOLK IP12 1DS, UK
TELEPHONE: 01394 385501 FACSIMILE: 01394 384434
or
MARKET STREET INDUSTRIAL PARK, WAPPINGERS' FALLS, NY 12590, USA
TELEPHONE: (914) 297 0003 FACSIMILE: (914) 297 0068
Email address: INFO@ANTIQUECC.COMp://www.antiquecc.com

This is an uncommon Derby figure of Saint Thomas, 10¼in. (26cm) high. dating from the late 1750s, yet it sold for only £280 at Phillips in June 1996. Age, maker and rarity are all important, but if a subject is unattractive, most collectors will not want to own it.

The same subject made at the same factory, but nearly two centuries apart. This fish seller from the Cris de Paris series was first made in the 1740s and the 18th century example modelled by Reinicke (left) is exciting, while the 20th century version has lost all of the magic. 5¼in. (13.5cm).

sentiment in its place. The best way is to decide to raise enough money to buy one good item and then pull out of your cabinets the pieces you feel least attached to up to the value of the object in question. Sell them all in one go and once you have received the proceeds spend it on something that will enhance the collection. I knew one collector who had a periodic weed-out of a quarter of his collection so that he could start afresh and really enjoy going out buying. Drastic perhaps, but in many ways this makes a lot of sense.

As you enjoy porcelain and become a collector, your knowledge will inevitably grow. No one ever stops learning and there are plenty of specialist dealers willing to guide you. Never be afraid to ask. It is vital that you learn as much as you can, in order properly to appreciate the pieces that you own.

Specialist study weekends are one of the best ways to learn as well as an important means of meeting fellow collectors. Interesting lectures are organised by London dealers and salerooms and there are local as well as national collectors' clubs. I spend a great deal of my own spare time travelling all over the country sharing my enthusiasm with keen audiences.

Reading provides the important stories behind the porcelain itself, and I have given details of many excellent general books in the bibliography. Specialist works are listed under the section on each principal factory, although many classic works are sadly out of print. It is well worth visiting specialist ceramic book dealers to obtain as much literature as you can on your chosen area of collecting. Armed with this, porcelain cannot fail to give you pleasure.

CHAPTER 2

Bargain Hunting and Serious Searching

While all collectors dream about dis- covering an incredible rarity in a junk shop or at a car boot sale, in reality there is more chance of finding a real bargain at a big antiques fair where there is a greater choice. The knack is pitting your wits and specialist knowledge against the dealers, hoping that you know something they don't. Fabulous finds can be made at boot fairs, but mostly in the area of 1950s and '60s memorabilia. Most 'Booters' who sell at such events watch the BBC Antiques Roadshow and check in their Price Guides the value of everything.

The antiques business is unique in that it thrives on competition. The more antique shops there are in a town, the more likely collectors will travel there. The trade has changed in twenty years. Many shops have

shut for good and the dealers are trading just as well with the smaller overheads of a booth in an antiques centre or at one-day antiques fairs. In a way this is sad, but it is still possible to build a friendship with a specialist dealer in an antiques market or at regular fairs.

Porcelain collectors treat dealers in different ways. To some they are almost like a secret enemy and a great game is played pretending not to show interest in an item, hoping the dealer will not realise the buyer knows what he is looking at. This can result in a reduced price, but if a dealer specialises in something you collect, it is far better to build up a friendly relationship so that the dealer will keep things for you. Dealers work very hard scouring the country for fresh stock to supply their many different collectors, and favoured customers

Hunting at a car boot sale can be rewarding, but it is necessary to sift through an awful lot of junk.

always get first refusal as long as they pay the asking price. Dealers who specialise in a certain type of porcelain are usually very knowledgeable. You will normally pay a higher price buying from a specialist, but in return you get the satisfaction of a virtual guarantee that an item is authentic. Dealers will guide collectors away from poor and inferior pieces as part of the pride they get in helping form a good private collection.

Collectors need to feel satisfied that they are not being overcharged, and it is important to look at the stock of other dealers and follow prices in auction rooms, as some specialist dealers do work on a very high mark-up. This is often due to the high costs of shop premises in London where most specialists are based. Also the cost of a stand at a prestigious antiques fair is considerable. It is no good begrudging a dealer his profit, as he has a living to make. The secret here is shopping around and learning what the right price should be. Good dealer-collector friendships soon come to an end if customers feel they are being exploited.

There are many points to remember when buying from dealers. Firstly, never trust dealers who do not clearly label their stock and won't volunteer information about the items they are selling. Even in the antiques trade you have your rights and legislation is there to protect you if you buy something that turns out to be not as described. Local Trading Standards officials can investigate complaints, but you must have a receipt which states clearly what you have bought. Always ask for a receipt as, if for no other reason, this is your protection if a piece you buy turns out to have been stolen. A receipt should describe the item, give the approximate date of manufacture, and also list any damage or restoration. This is the biggest single cause of complaint in the antique porcelain business. Always ask a dealer 'Has this been restored?' A reputable dealer will not be offended, and will be glad to offer reassurance. He knows the restoration of porcelain is widespread and will understand a collector's caution. It goes without saying that any dealer who will not give such a receipt should not be trusted.

If you are in any way suspicious, always seek a second opinion. Take your purchase along to an auction room or to another antiques fair and ask other dealers. Specialist ceramic fairs often have an expert on hand to give verbal opinions and appraisals. These are usually free, but a small charge is money well spent for peace of mind. Auctioneers are not really a free valuation service and their busy experts are there to advise customers wanting to sell through them. As an auction expert I do not mind advising collectors occasionally, just as long as they are straight with me and tell me why they are after a second opinion. Remember, though, that every expert will have a different idea of the value of an object and do not feel too let down if they estimate less than you have paid. What you are seeking is agreement on an attribution.

Specialised ceramic fairs have become an established tradition in Britain and are certainly good for the trade. Any rivalry between dealers at a fair is usually very friendly. They may be selling similar stock and have outbid each other to buy pieces at auctions, but all benefit from the attraction of the event which will bring more customers to a dealer's stand in one day than would visit a shop in a whole year. These fairs bring together a quite considerable amount of fine porcelain and collectors have the opportunity of comparing prices of similar things on sale with different dealers.

Long queues build up at the opening of major fairs, for exhibitors will be offering for the first time pieces they may have bought over several months. As a result there can be something resembling a rugby scrum in front of popular dealers' stands when the doors open for the first time. Decisions to buy expensive objects have to be made instantly, and many collectors live to regret rash purchases made in the heat of the moment.

Many fairs are 'vetted' by a panel made up of exhibitors and external consultants, usually from museums. The purpose is to weed out obvious forgeries and wrong attributions, but buyers have little redress to the organisers of a fair in the event of a complaint and you should still get a receipt from the individual dealer. Porcelain usually looks wonderful under the bright lights of an antiques fair, but it is

Porcelain for sale at the annual International Ceramics Fair and Seminar each June at The Park Lane Hotel, London.

important to remember that a lot of pieces will have been professionally restored so that they look their best. It is up to the buyer to be suspicious and ask if restoration has taken place.

Auctioneers' catalogues are full of small print apparently disclaiming all responsibility, but even so the buyer has plenty of rights and the same Trading Standards legislation to fall back on. An important point to remember is that you cannot expect the general antiques cataloguers in a small provincial saleroom to have the same expertise as a major London or New York gallery. This usually works to the advantage of collectors who visit Victoriana and bric-à-brac sales in the hope that they know more than anyone else there.

Bargains are not necessarily all that they seem, however. More reproduction (i.e. fake) antiques are sold by auction in Britain than by traders openly dealing in reproductions. Wholesale importers sell the latest forgeries from the Far East to middlemen who consign them to any auction room that will take them. Often these are taken to the salerooms by little old ladies and the auction staff do not suspect they are modern Taiwanese copies. Mostly, however, the porters on duty in a saleroom have a jolly good idea which lots are fakes, and it is well worth asking.

The British public are funny when they go into an auction room. They seem to think they are being 'watched' and that if they show undue interest in something they are convinced they will be 'run-up' and made to pay more as a result. Nothing can be further from the truth, and on the whole the specialists in an auction room are more than happy to answer any questions about the lots on sale. They may not be knowledgeable enough to confirm which factory made a particular vase, but they will usually be able to tell you if a piece is restored or a modern reproduction.

There is much criticism levelled at auctioneers for the charges they make, especially to buyers. The buyers' premium is a fixed amount payable on the selling price (the 'hammer price' at which a lot is knocked down). This ranges from 5% to 15% and should be clearly stated in the auction catalogue. The premium is a fact of life and a necessity to cover the overheads of running the business, just as a dealer works a profit margin into his selling price. But with VAT payable on the buyers' premium too, this is a sizeable amount to pay on top of the price you actually bid and it must be taken into account when you work out the sum you want to bid up to. Buyers in small country auctions may legitimately wonder what they get for their premium, with a brief or even misleading catalogue and often very little expertise to back it up. The situation is very different in a major saleroom where the catalogue is often a significant work of reference and the specialists are respected as among the most knowledgeable people in their field.

Writing as a Bond Street specialist with twenty years' experience cataloguing at Phillips, I am often surprised how rarely I am consulted by private buyers who are probably dying to know more about a piece of porcelain they are thinking of bidding on. My catalogue gives a full description and date for each item and lists any damage, restoration or other defects, so it is mostly all there in black and white. Anyone can ask to speak with one of the specialists, however, and it is well worth having a discussion. 'Do you think it is a good example of its type?' 'How rare is it?' 'Will I find a better example easily or is it worth paying a bit more for this one?' 'Is the estimate realistic or have you been over-cautious?' An auctioneer naturally will not tell you what the reserve is, or what other bids have already been left, in the same way that he would never disclose your bids to anyone else. This position of trust is most important, but I fully understand that not every auctioneer can be trusted and buyers are naturally suspicious. Salerooms are not the exclusive domain of the dealer any more and private buyers are vital to the success of all major auctioneers. For this reason the catalogues have become more

glossy, resembling a brochure, and sales are laid out more in 'interiors' settings than museum cabinets. Anyone can view an auction sale. There is no entry fee although you may have to give some identity. It is therefore possible to visit central London, New York, Geneva or Hong Kong and handle some of the world's greatest porcelain for yourself. This is surely the best way to learn, for the catalogue tells you all you need to know and you can come and watch the sale and note the selling prices.

With the private competition nowadays, auction prices are not necessarily cheaper than you would have to pay at a specialist dealer. It might be argued that a dealer has to make his profit and that if you outbid a dealer in a saleroom you will still be paying less than you would have to pay in his shop. This is true, but dealers are often prepared to pay over the odds for something they really want and you may find you are not the only one who gets carried away with auction fever. If you bid more than you intended to there is no redress, so you really have to set yourself a limit of the total price you want to pay. A lot of collectors prefer to ask a friendly dealer to bid in person for them, paying him a commission of maybe 10 or 20% for his assistance and advice. If you buy at auction yourself and the lot you bought turns out to be not as described, you are entitled to a full refund in most cases. If damage is not listed in a catalogue there is no comeback if a lot turns out to be restored unless you requested a written 'condition report' before the sale. It is always worth asking for this, but don't leave it to the last minute.

Many collectors fear getting carried away bidding in a saleroom and prefer to leave a written 'commission' bid with the auction firm. This is normally given to the auctioneer who controls the bidding and who will buy a lot as cheaply as possible allowing for the reserve and other bids in the room. This totally depends on trust, and in practice most auctioneers are totally honest with commission bids – their reputation is too important to put on the line for the sake of a few false bids. This is not necessarily the case in all countries and overseas buyers like to bid by telephone during

In the excitement of a sale, an auctioneer is faced with a sea of faces, but experience rarely if ever misses a bid.

the sale. This adds excitement to a major auction and is not without its dangers as telephone lines sometimes break down. It is only possible to bid by telephone for expensive items and if you are a regular buyer.

It is frustrating when a collector thinks he has found something exciting in an out-of-the-way saleroom, or foreign country even, only to discover that all the dealers who specialise in this kind of porcelain have heard about it also. Modern technology has replaced the role of the traditional dealers' 'runners' who travelled the country seeking rarities in country sales and tipping off the London trade for a fee. Nowadays computers can scan auction catalogues, and for a single subscription to an auction-search service collectors can be advised by Fax of items of interest in sales all over the world. There is still the chance of finding a 'sleeper' – a lot that is wrongly catalogued and overlooked – but if a piece of Meissen or Worcester is in a sale anywhere

from Aberdeen to Barnstaple, the specialist dealers get to hear.

In these modern times details of sales are broadcast on the Internet, and many dealers are now buying pages on the 'Web' to sell porcelain and other antiques to a whole new generation of collectors. Computer records of past sales replace the need for libraries of catalogues to use for research. Dealers keep their stock on computer, and collectors can buy special software to record their collections and update their own catalogue and insurance. Progress is fast, but thankfully most porcelain collectors remain old fashioned and still collect by the more traditional means. They enjoy having their collections around them and sharing them with others at their local antique collectors' club. Sometimes as much swapping and trading goes on among fellow collectors at a members' evening as at a busy antiques fair. This sort of collecting is probably more fun than anything.

CHAPTER 3

Fakes, Reproductions and Restoration

Forgery is so widespread in the world of antiques that there is barely a category of porcelain that has not attracted the attention of fakers. I viewed a recent local antiques auction and noted that one sixth of all the porcelain in the sale was modern, mostly fakes made in Taiwan or China. In the sale there were no less than two Ming dishes which ought to be worth at least £200,000 each if real. No one in their right mind was going to believe these in a little sale in Kent, but the fake Staffordshire figures and Art Deco vases were attracting considerable interest.

Deception comes in many forms. There are blatant copies made to fool experts, but also grey areas such as reproductions made quite legitimately to replace types of porcelain no longer available. Re-decoration changes the appearance of things that were old fashioned so that they could be sold – no less honest perhaps than modern repairs which hide unsightly

damage. A copy may well have been sold openly as a reproduction when it was made, but if it deceives collectors today then it must be classed as a fake.

Porcelain has been faked since early times, when Persian potters copied Yuan and Ming dishes traded along the Silk Road. In the seventeenth century Delft vases were essentially fakes of Chinese porcelain, and the Chinese themselves made exact copies of fifteenth century porcelain, complete with Ming marks, three hundred years later. Today we do not think of early Chelsea or Bow copies of Chinese porcelain as fakes, but in London in 1750 some customers must have bought Bow teasets from china shops thinking they had come from the Far East, not from East London. Some early English copies of Chinese blue and white are today worth twenty times as much as the Chinese original would be. It is a curious state of affairs, but any copy made in the eighteenth

This modern Chinese dish would be worth a small fortune if it was a genuine early Ming example. Such pieces regularly turn up in antique markets and salerooms in the west, but for less than £100 who on earth is going to think they are buying the real thing?

This authentic Sèvres plate was originally painted only with simple flowers. The turquoise ground and extra festoons were added in the 19th century. Close examination reveals signs of refiring, especially scratches which 'disappear' under added decoration.

This tiny early 20th century tiger in hard paste porcelain reproduced a Meissen original. The genuine maker's mark, of the Samson factory, has been removed from the base in a later unscrupulous attempt to deceive. Note the patch of missing glaze where the mark has been ground away.

century is today regarded as a genuine collector's item, while any copy made in the nineteenth century is condemned as a fake.

Fake porcelain in the modern sense began in the 1820s when old Sèvres was commanding high sums. Lavish wares made before the French Revolution were very valuable in England and were copied in London. Instead of trying to reproduce the beautiful soft-paste of Sèvres, china dealers in London imported chests full of old white-glazed Sèvres porcelain which had been stored in a warehouse at the Sèvres factory since before the Revolution. Most had only slight faults but had been discarded during manufacture. This was painted in London with careful copies of early Sèvres bird and flower painting and sumptuous coloured grounds. Sold at the time as genuine eighteenth century Sèvres, some of this re-decorated porcelain has been passed down in families for more than 150 years. It is hard to convince some owners today that what they really have are elaborate hoaxes.

Old porcelain was keenly collected in Victorian times and often quite valuable. Early Chelsea, Meissen and Worcester changed hands for high sums, while Chinese Kangxi porcelain was worth a fortune. The best known and certainly the most prolific forger of all time was the Paris firm of Edmé Samson and Cie. They were never prosecuted for they claimed that they never made fakes, only reproductions which were sold openly as such. This is

probably correct, but no doubt they were happy to sell to unscrupulous dealers who passed off the best Samson very easily to unsuspecting Victorian gentlemen. Samson's own marks and tell-tale mould numbers have often been ground off the back or base of a Samson forgery, and this was done for only one reason. I have been caught out on many occasions myself by clever Samson copies, and I know of very reputable dealers who have likewise been tricked into parting with considerable sums for supposedly Chelsea scent bottles and Meissen figures. Some Samson fakes can be detected using ultraviolet light, for traces of uranium added to the glaze on some models causes the surface to fluoresce a brilliant yellow. Most Samson does not glow in this way, however, and it is more a matter of experience, learning what to look for and the incorrect tone of Samson's very white porcelain body. The wrong body can be the biggest giveaway, for Samson porcelain uses kaolin and is a true hard paste, whereas Chelsea, Bow and Worcester ought to be soft paste with a very different appearance. It takes years of experience to tell the difference between hard and soft paste, and never let anyone tell you it's easy.

Everyone has heard of Samson, but how many people know of Reginald Newland? He worked with Gerald Moore at Torquay, Devon, trading as 'Creative Studios'. During the 1950s very clever fakes began to appear all over the country in the style of Bow, Derby and

Although purporting to be Chelsea, this pair of Continental figures owes more to decorative Dresden traditions than early English. The gold anchor mark is easy to copy, but whereas Chelsea hid their marks discreetly, the faker placed his in an over prominent position on the back of the model. c.1920.

Longton Hall. When exposed Newland and Moore also claimed that their models were only ever sold as 'the finest quality repros.', but many had fetched considerable sums. One original customer who sold Newland's repro. Staffordshire cottages told me that they came with instructions for ageing (place Gum Arabic in the corners and insert into the hoover bag!). Most 'Torquay' fakes copied known models, but some were excellent pastiches combining elements from different originals. The cottages are crude and hard to take seriously, but I am frequently amazed at the ingenuity of the best

A 'Torquay' figure made as a pastiche of Bow, Chelsea and Meissen. As such it is a particularly clever fake, for it cannot be compared with any existing original. 1950s.   Private collection

Harlequin groups. Owners of Newland's work rarely admit to having been fooled and forever argue that other experts are wrong.

It is interesting to hear of the original instructions for 'ageing' Torquay fakes. It is usually bad attempts at ageing that provide us with the best clues with which to condemn fakes. Modern copies made in the Orient arrive in England caked with a kind of sticky black gravy which I am told is shoe blacking. The application of this liquid dirt is usually so unconvincing I find it laughable, but several inexperienced collectors have brought to me at

BBC Antiques Roadshows Japanese cats or Chinese fishbowls that they have bought in auctions and spent hours lovingly scrubbing to clean off the 'old dirt'. Without the fake ageing they look brand new, but still some folk stubbornly refuse to believe me. I have seen some really excellent late nineteenth century copies of Delft and Meissen porcelain which, had they not been subjected to fake ageing, would probably have fooled me too. Some forgers assumed that their copies would look too new and so they attacked their creations with scouring pads or sandpaper. Old porcelain does get scratched, but only on exposed parts underneath the base or on the widest part where it will have rubbed against a wall. A china figure with scuffing among the folds of the costume or under a separate arm can only be a fake for a genuine figure would never have suffered intense wear in such inaccessible areas.

Small details were often overlooked by forgers and allow us to detect their work. Genuine Sèvres porcelain was hung during the glaze firing on a metal hook inserted in a hole in the footrim. Copyists knew this and made sure they added a footrim hole to their pieces too. The original Sèvres holes did not fill with glaze but instead have traces of a black deposit left by the spike which stuck into the hole during the firing. The holes on many of the fakes are neat and clean and filled with glaze, and so served no purpose when the plates were made. They cannot therefore be genuine Sèvres.

It is impossible in this guide to mention all of the fakes that I know about and of course there must be many that I haven't yet heard about. The best modern fakes from China of Imperial Qing porcelain are so incredibly clever it is likely that some must remain undetected even by top experts. The implication of modern technology is frightening. Colour printing on porcelain is so advanced that any painting can be reproduced on a cheap plate to sell for less than £10 in magazine advertisements. The same processes have been used to make fake Berlin plaques that exactly reproduce, by photographic means, a nineteenth century original. The porcelain looks new and Oriental and the 'painting' is made up of very tiny dots of colour

This cup and saucer, sold at Phillips in 1995, was believed to be perfect, but when the Japanese buyer came to use it, he found it had been broken and very cleverly restored. Phillips arranged a full refund and stood the loss when the piece, catalogued as restored, was resold for much less.

rather than brush-strokes. Placed in old frames, however, some of these have sold for hundreds of pounds. Within a few years no doubt the photographic processes will be further advanced and it will be impossible to see the microscopic dots. What then?

It is no use collecting and enjoying antique porcelain if you are terrified of buying a fake. It is easy for me to write that the only way to avoid fakes is to learn everything you can about the genuine thing, but I realise such expertise is not within everyone's reach. It is too often repeated that you cannot be caught out if you buy only from reputable dealers or major auctioneers who offer guarantees, but even the best of us will be caught out some time. The guarantee that such a reputation offers is significant, however, for when a major saleroom is informed that it has sold a fake, the purchaser is normally refunded without question. Specialist dealers likewise value their reputations and will

usually make good any losses. Happily, considering the size of the collectors' market, fake porcelain is not a major problem.

Restoration has become a much greater headache for porcelain collectors. As professional restorers become ever more skilful, it is increasingly difficult to tell when and to what extent a piece of porcelain has been restored. Many restorers prefer to be called conservators and their talents are used by museums to prevent cracks extending or unstable decoration from deteriorating. Porcelain which has stained often quite badly can be chemically cleaned to return it to its original appearance, and heavy wear and unsightly damage can be disguised so that a sad-looking specimen can be put proudly on display. From this museum-type perspective porcelain restoration is to be very much encouraged.

Ordinary people have been using repairers since the eighteenth century. Any porcelain that was broken was taken to a 'China Burner' who used a special enamel to melt broken porcelain back together again. An alternative method was riveting by which broken porcelain was stitched back together using tiny red-hot rivets. Riveting continued until the 1950s when strong glues finally became available. The Victorians used other methods to restore porcelain including drastic overpainting. All collectors today will be familiar with the appearance of aged restoration which has to be stripped off to reveal what lies underneath.

Modern restoration really can make broken porcelain look as good as new. I encourage the work of good modern restorers, although not all auctioneers and collectors share this view. It is all a question of moderation. Restoration that disguises unsightly damage is good, as an ugly crack will totally spoil the beauty of a fine object. If a hand is missing from a figurine or the knop missing from a teapot, the charm of the piece is completely lost. A simple repair can transform a sad-looking object into something that can be enjoyed once more and this is fine. What I cannot condone is restoration just for its own sake. A fine crack that can hardly be seen, or other damage that is not obtrusive in any way, is better left alone than hidden under a sea of synthetic varnish. Artificial glazes do not have the same feel as the cold surface of fine porcelain, so that if a piece is fully sprayed over, it no longer feels like a real piece of old porcelain.

It is clear that every collector views restoration in a different way. Collectors who want to have a prized piece fully restored to their own taste are welcome to do so, just as long as the repair does not cost more than the damaged piece is actually worth. Make no mistake, no matter how skilful the restoration is, a repaired piece is not worth the same as a perfect one.

This is so important when you are buying restored porcelain. If a dealer tells you that a piece you are considering has 'had a little repair', ask questions and try to find out exactly what has happened to it. Slight cosmetic repair to extremities is fine, but if a piece has been completely broken it is a different matter. Imagine the restoration taken away. Would you still want to buy a plate that has been in four pieces? Repairs will not last for ever and you are basically buying a damaged piece of porcelain. The price you are asked has to reflect this. Even if you have good eyesight, don't ever think you can always spot if a piece has been restored. I would challenge anyone not to be able to detect some repairs I have seen. The dealer or auctioneer selling a piece may not know it has been restored, but ask for a condition report anyway and hold them to it. If you discover at home later that there is repair that was not disclosed, take it straight back and demand a refund.

Most porcelain is repaired in obvious places. With figures it is the neck or fingers that usually break. The spout of a teapot or lip of a jug are vulnerable parts so look closely. Remember porcelain is translucent, and while a repairer can cover up any crack, put a light bulb behind it and the crack appears right back again. Some people tap the surface of porcelain with their teeth or a pin to detect the soft feel of varnish, but this practice should not be encouraged as it can scratch what might have been a very costly repair. Ultraviolet light will show differences in surface texture through the colour of fluorescence, but you do need complete darkness, the right kind of lamp and experience in knowing what to look for. Do not rely on being able to spot repair yourself. Ask the seller first, and if in doubt get a second opinion.

CHAPTER 4

Displaying and Caring for your Collection

Royal Worcester's Japanesque porcelain of the 1870s cleverly reproduced the new styles from Japan. Victorian collectors would have placed this on Oriental style hardwood furniture in mock Japanese interiors. Today a collection like this can be displayed to suit any taste, modern or traditional.

One of the nice things about collecting porcelain is that it needs very little looking after, although it does not take too kindly to bumps and knocks. The magic of fire has fused shape, glaze and decoration together in a union that should last to eternity. Porcelain is there to be enjoyed, and a quick rub over with a duster is usually all it needs to keep your collection presentable.

Many pieces will benefit from a good clean. Porcelain that has been neglected can look sad, but it doesn't take much to transform some pieces and at the same time increase the value. The best thing is a simple wash with nothing stronger than soft soap or washing-up liquid. An old toothbrush will help clean awkward

shapes, while a child's paintbrush can get gently into delicate places to dislodge dust and dirt. Rinse well with clean water and leave to dry by itself rather than use a rough towel. Avoid immersing hollow cast items, for these have tiny blowholes hidden away to let air escape during firing. A figure group can leak water from these tiny holes for weeks afterwards all over your antique furniture.

If a piece of porcelain is white or has underglaze decoration only, a more intense scrub using a non-abrasive cream cleaner is quite safe and will remove dirt from ugly surface scratches. With great care some enamelled decoration can be cleaned in a similar way, but never use cleaning agents on

Minton and Coalport trompe l'œil *dishes look magnificent on a side table, but would never survive regular dusting. A display cabinet free of dust is the only practical way to display very delicate porcelain.*

items with gilding. Gold really will come straight off. In cases of severe staining, chemical cleaning is possible, but I cannot recommend anyone to attempt this themselves. Peroxide can be applied carefully, using cloth soaked in a concentrated solution, to draw discoloration out from within the body of the china. Many dealers swear by their own methods and special solutions (including a popular brand of nappy cleaner), but such action is best left to professionals. Never use bleach, as most household bleaches severely affect ceramic bodies and glazes. They may look fine to begin with, but some weeks after bleach treatment tell-tale purple discoloration occurs, especially round gilding. A white powder of tiny crystals may form on the surface followed by flaking of the glaze. If you are offered a piece which seems to have white fur growing on it, don't assume it has just been stored in a damp cellar. You may find later the glaze falls off in lumps.

If porcelain has slight damage you can consider a sympathetic restoration by professionals. It is up to your own taste and, as I mentioned in the previous chapter, I encourage

good restoration where damage is unsightly. Most repairers will, if asked, carry out a 'museum-type' restoration without using a spray. You will still be able to see the damage when you look closely, but your eye is not immediately drawn to an ugly break. Always keep the cost of any repair in perspective as good restorers are expensive.

Displaying your porcelain is a very personal thing. Collectors' club meetings often debate the merits of whether to cram or not to cram. Porcelain can be safe in a display cabinet away from dust and little fingers, but it is hard to appreciate the beauty of individual pieces. It is important that a collection is accessible, as one of the joys of porcelain is to hold it and feel it. Space is often a problem, and a collection has to fit within the confines of your home. What must be avoided is placing items close to any source of heat, and this can include lights in display cabinets. Although it will have been fired at high temperature, porcelain does expand and contract slightly with changes in temperature. Rapid changes will causes stress resulting in crazing or actual cracks. Never place porcelain on a windowsill. It may get

1930s Royal Worcester bird models by Eva Soper and a 1960s teaset by Daisy Rea, displayed happily together on antique shelves
Sandon collection

cool at night and then can heat up very rapidly if the sun shines directly on to it. Take great care also if you buy something at a house sale in a marquee or at an outdoor antiques market. If you take it straight home and put it in on warm lit display shelves, it may suddenly go 'ping' as it cracks!

There is no denying porcelain looks great on antique furniture, ideally of the same period as the porcelain itself – Chinese Chippendale hanging shelves for eighteenth century figurines, a Japanesque dark wood cabinet for Victorian porcelain, and an Art Deco display cabinet for 1920s Doulton. This is fine if you live in a house that suits such furniture, and many collectors choose porcelain of the same period as their home. Eighteenth century display cabinets are terribly costly, but well made Edwardian reproductions are fine for porcelain. Always check the safety of cabinet shelves regularly. I have advised on many insurance claims for porcelain broken by warping wood or deteriorated shelf fixings.

I find that antique furniture does not live comfortably in modern houses. There is no reason why old porcelain should not be displayed on modern units, however. America has realised this. In home furnishing stores across the States you can choose from a great range of metal and glass etagères, but in Britain such items are normally only sold as shop fittings. Think how good porcelain looks on modern illuminated units at an antiques fair and then ask yourself if such a display would suit your house. I have heard collectors grumble that an expensive purchase looked wonderful at a fair but was disappointing when taken home. Most likely the problem is poor lighting. Bright spotlights transform dull shelves into a stunning display. Colourful porcelain needs plenty of light, and stylish figurines like to cast strong shadows.

In the eighteenth century many great houses had their 'China Room' lined with wall-to-wall blue and white Chinese porcelain. Following the success of the 'Nankin Cargo' and other high-profile shipwreck sales in Amsterdam, this sort of display has come back into fashion again, and is certainly a stunning way to show off blue and white porcelain. Also dinner services make a great display hung on a kitchen wall. Contrary to many peoples' views, porcelain plates can be hung safely on a wall. The key is to use plastic-coated hanging wires of exactly the right size, as these won't cause chips. If a plate is cracked, though, the crack should be sealed first with a permanent adhesive. Old bent wire hangers should be cut off plates using a hack-saw, as forcing them off usually causes chipping. Never use the disc type of hangers which are glued on the back of a plate as these can strip the glaze from crazed porcelain. Also, if you hang heavy plates or dishes make sure you check the nail or screw is firmly in the wall, preferably with a wallplug, as again this is a common cause of insurance claims.

For insurance reasons it is vital that any collection of antiques is valued regularly and a detailed inventory kept complete with photographs. Records should include exact measurements and note any distinguishing markings or damage. In the event of a burglary, photo-graphs circulated to dealers and auction rooms often lead to recovery of stolen antiques. Valuation fees and insurance premiums can be expensive and it is worth shopping around. Sadly too many collectors say to me they cannot afford to insure their collections at today's values, and they often have cause to regret this in the long run.

The police recommend all households mark their property with the postcode written using an invisible pen. While I support this policy in principal, so called 'invisible' markings are not hard to see and can be harmful, especially to unglazed porcelain or to any china that is crazed on the surface. The marking sinks into the body and can never be removed, and I have noticed some collectors are reluctant to buy items disfigured with such indelible marks. Only write your postcode on porcelain that has a smooth, unblemished glaze and try to write small.

CHAPTER 5

What is available within your Price Range

Under £50. A selection of egg cups, 19th and 20th century. Examples like these cost no more than a few pounds.
Sandon collection

UNDER £50

While experts on BBC's Antiques Road-show always seem to talk about valuable rarities, there is still plenty of opportunity for a beginner to get started. Elsewhere in this guide I advocate buying the best that you can afford, but it is important to start out in a simple way and have fun collecting at the same time.

Collecting porcelain under £50 means one of two things. You can buy damaged examples or odd bits of fine porcelain — a great way to learn — or else you can collect an object or type that is plentiful and thus inexpensive. What you must avoid is buying a bad example of something just because it is cheap.

The egg cups on this page are part of my young daughter's collection, all picked up at car boot sales. Elizabeth has over two hundred and the most expensive cost £5. Admittedly, most of her collection is relatively modern, but within this price range it does not matter. Disney characters are already keenly sought, and in years to come no doubt the Power Rangers will epitomise the 1990s just as Noddy and the Magic Roundabout were heroes in the '60s and '70s. A number of Victorian china egg cups have cost no more than modern ones – 10p to 50p is the usual price Elizabeth pays. If you can't face boot fairs, specialist dealers will charge you between £10 and £50 for Victorian porcelain egg cups, and it is possible to specialise – Crested China or souvenir scenic views for instance. Eighteenth

Under £50. A German porcelain plate with photo-litho decoration and printed gold, c.1890. Attractive plates that are well printed can cost only £20-£40.
Sandon collection

Under £50. Badly damaged, but £45 instead of £600 and a super example from which to learn. The quality of Worcester's overglaze printing is not affected by the damage. c.1757. Sandon collection

century examples cost hundreds of pounds, but all collectors need something to aspire to. There is even a name for collecting egg cups – *Pocillovy*.

Thimbles present another opportunity with plenty of new ones available for less than £10, but it is much harder to find antique china thimbles and these are generally very expensive.

Most European porcelain of quality is out of this price range, as hand-decoration was always costly, but one area worth looking at is the best of photo-litho printing. I do not mean new 'collectors' plates' particularly, although if bought second-hand these can be cheap. Seek out instead the best German and Bohemian colour printing of the 1890s and 1900s. Porcelain marked 'R S Prussia' and 'Royal Bayreuth' is already keenly collected in the United States, but this is an area yet to catch on in Britain. For fine hand painting at an inexpensive price you must look to Japan and the eggshell tea and coffee sets which are so abundant. They were cheap in the 1920s and '30s and every home bought them, so they are plentiful today and totally neglected. Most were mass-produced with no care at all, but the best – and I only suggest buying top quality

examples – are superbly painted, elegant and decorative. Cups and saucers can be found for a few pounds each and make a splendid display.

Many collectors will buy only perfect porcelain, and of course I understand this attitude. For educational purposes, however, damaged wrecks can provide a wonderful chance to learn and the means to own some of the world's rarest porcelain for as little as £20-£50. An eighteenth century Meissen plate that might cost £600 in good condition will be £30 if it has been broken in half. A very broken eighteenth century English teabowl can be bought for just a few pounds, but will have all the characteristics of shape, glaze, colours and translucency of a perfect example. Damaged pieces are no use as teaching guides if they have been restored, as overpainting hides original glaze, so it is essential to strip off any old repair. Odd lids can teach a great deal and also make an interesting and decorative collection. Many antique dealers have a box of odd lids tucked away somewhere left over from teasets. They hope that one day they might match one up with its pot, but they never do and can usually be persuaded to part with them for just a few pounds.

£50-£100

In antique collecting terms, nice porcelain can seem remarkably reasonable. For £100 you can buy a jolly nice piece from the nineteenth century and even earlier china can cost under £100 if you are not too fussy. The trick here is to look for odd cups, single plates and other simple shapes from teasets. Single cups and saucers are the most widely collected of all porcelain items. The scope here is almost endless – pretty German or French *demi-tasses* from the 1910s and '20s; striking Art Deco from Doulton or Shelley; elaborate early Victorian specimens from over-the-top tea services; older teabowls and saucers from Paris, New Hall and other Staffordshire makers at the end of the eighteenth century; and even Chinese blue and white cups and saucers of fifty years earlier still. Purpose-made stands can display collections of cups and saucers beautifully, and for that special occasion mixed collections of cups and saucers can mostly still be used for their original purpose of serving coffee or tea.

If your attraction is for the eighteenth century or you like richer decoration, then in this price band you must stick to single cups without saucers. This really is a very big field indeed and it is important to be discerning. You must choose cups that stand up as quality items by themselves, or are interesting in some way. Pleasant eighteenth century cups from Meissen, Worcester and Derby frequently cost less than £100 and some beautifully decorated Chinese coffee cups are incredibly reasonable. Some collectors stick to coffee cans, as they do look very nice together in a display – consequently a straight-sided can will generally cost three times the price of a coffee cup of the same pattern. Teapots have many collectors and mostly fall into the next price band over £100. Milk jugs and covered sugar bowls from the same services are usually much cheaper, and many nice examples can be picked up for £70-£100. Plates take up more room than cups and saucers, but if you have plenty of wall space a display of Victorian dessert plates can be most attractive. Plates come in all price ranges, of course, but for £60-£80 good quality examples by less well-known makers offer the best value around. Avoid plates that are rubbed and worn, however, as these will always look sad as part of a display.

Ornamental pieces by reasonable makers are generally more costly, but for between £50 and £100 it is possible to buy pieces that are still well made and pretty, but by less well-known makers. Prices for bisque porcelain figurines from France and Germany start at around £40. It is hard to tell how old some of them are, and some were made very cheaply, so it is

£50-£100. One of the most popular areas of porcelain collecting. Cups and saucers are quaint to display and represent so well the work of different makers.

£50-£100. Popular German 'Bisque' figurines start from as little as £50 a pair and rarely cost more than £200 complete with glass domes. Although hardly Works of Art, most have given pleasure to their owners over many generations. 7¼in. (18.5cm).

Sandon collection

£50-£100. You cannot compare Chinese vases from 1900 with originals two centuries older, but hand painted to traditional designs, late examples are still jolly decorative and often cost a lot less than £100.

£50-£100. China animals can be expensive if made by Worcester or Meissen, but cheaper examples, made by nobody in particular, can still make a fun collection. Pugs are a popular breed for porcelain collectors.

important to use a bit of discretion and avoid figures with little colouring and poor definition. It is possible to put together collections of certain types of ornament. Fairings – the titled German novelty groups supposedly given as fairground prizes – can be bought in specialist collectors' sales for well under £100 each, unless the subject is particularly rare. The little china ladies that sat on pincushions or tea cosies early this century are another growing area of collecting, but again watch out for fakes. Animals are popular, and many young collectors start by hunting china models of their favourites. Cats are very sought after, as are frogs and, more surprisingly, pigs. A whole range of so-called 'Pig Fairings' were made in Germany eighty years ago and these are now quite expensive. This sort of collecting can become compulsive and it is essential to keep one eye on quality. Animal models by some major factories, such as Meissen, Doulton and Worcester, are mostly over £100 each now, but other makers such as Rosenthal and Crown Staffordshire are more reasonable. A wide range of porcelain animals made in Soviet Russia are very appealing and have much potential as collectors' items. Most collectors have limited space, and so little animal models

are obviously popular for this reason. Chinese snuff bottles have a similar attraction. Rarities will be costly, but many nice late nineteenth century porcelain snuff bottles cost less than £100 and seem more reasonably priced than glass ones.

£100-£250

As collectors pay more for single pieces of porcelain, it is very important to focus on some kind of theme. This tends to be dictated by personal taste, and collectors choose either a period, a single maker or a single shape. Teapots are among the most popular shapes within this price range, although many fun teapots can be bought for less than £100. Because teapots are plentiful, and take up a lot of room, it is far better to buy fewer of better quality. Dealers who buy tea services frequently split them up and sell them as single cups and saucers. The teapot is always the prize and in an auction room collectors often rush up to a dealer who has just bought a teaset, asking for first refusal on the teapot. Variety is better than the monotonous effect of lots of teapots of the same shape, but it is also very interesting to study teapot shapes and learn to

£100-£250. Staffordshire cottage pastille burners are still generally inexpensive and the best porcelain examples from the 1840s and '50s are excellent value. Slight damage is quite acceptable.

£100-£250. Neo-classical patterns from Derby, Bristol and Worcester, 1775-1790. Collecting a single colour or style has enormous potential if you want to display your porcelain in an authentic period setting.

recognise the maker from slight differences in the shape of the handle or spout. Avoid teapots with damaged spouts, for there is nothing more distracting than the end of a spout missing.

Many other shapes can form fascinating collections within this price range. Candlesticks can light up a table or sideboard and Staffordshire cottage pastille burners can form a rustic village street. Single cups and saucers and plates are available for display at cheaper prices, but for £200-£250 very nice examples can be bought which reflect the richer end of a factory's output. Decoration can form the basis of a collection and if you live in an old house your collection can match the period and taste of its original owners. Empire and Regency taste is more expensive, but within this price range earlier neo-classical porcelain is affordable. The collection of green monochrome patterns illustrated will make a dramatic display in a room decorated to a similar palette. High Victorian taste is a more neglected area, and there is plenty of opportunity still to collect

'Japanesque' and Aesthetic Movement porcelain from the 1870s and '80s.

Blue and white is the most widely collected single decoration and many good pieces can be bought for up to £250. Printed teawares from Worcester and Caughley are reasonably priced and Continental blue and white from Tournai, Copenhagen, and even Meissen is quite cheap. Chinese blue and white is the best value of all, especially Qianlong export teawares and plates. Cracks reduce the value of Oriental porcelain greatly and for as little as £100-£200 it is possible to buy really nice Kangxi blue and white with honest but not disfiguring damage. Early Japanese Imari is dear, but nineteenth century vases and dishes in the bright Imari colours cost from as little as £100-£150 and are growing in popularity.

Figurines can be seriously collected within this price band. Eighteenth century figures have to be damaged to be as little as £250, but more modern collectables offer a great deal of scope. Most collectors choose a single factory

£100-£250. 20th century figurines are very popular with collectors and there is plenty of opportunity within this price range. These are from Royal Worcester's 'Children of the Nations' series by Freda Doughty.

– Royal Worcester, Royal Doulton and Royal Copenhagen in particular. The value is mostly determined by rarity, and scarce figures in production for only a short time will fetch large sums now. It should be remembered that most figures are only rare because they failed to appeal when they were made. The ones that sold in large numbers may be common, but these are usually the most delightful and the most representative of fashions at the time they were made. Well-decorated, i.e. earlier examples, of the common figures give a lot of pleasure at reasonable prices compared with modern figures in our china stores today. Decorative Dresden and other Continental figures tend to be valued according to size and some pleasant smaller figurines are good value under £200. Look out for figures with detachable heads that nod gently up and down. Very popular a hundred years ago, these have many enthusiastic collectors today as children always love them (see page 9).

£250-£500. Single pieces from richly gilded dessert services make a colourful display recreating the taste of Regency England for far less, in real terms, than they cost their original owners in 1815-25.

£250-£500

This is the range of the true enthusiast who loves porcelain and wants to form a worthwhile collection. Spending up to £500 on a single piece involves care, but for this sum you can buy an example of fine workmanship or a rarity that will certainly give pleasure. It is above the general price of ordinary pieces from tea and dinner services and into the area of 'cabinet' pieces, the name given to rich porcelains that were made to be shown off rather than to be used. When rich dessert sets are sold for prices in excess of £250 per piece, they are usually split up by dealers and collectors have the chance to buy a single dish or pair of plates to use as sumptuous decoration. Value is determined by richness and quality, and a decorative late

nineteenth century plate in the Sèvres or Vienna style will be worth more than a plain eighteenth century piece. Generally, vases and cups and saucers are preferred to plates, unless they have a very full painting in the centre.

Collectors can indulge in specific themes beyond a single factory. Blue and white collectors can specialise in fashionable shapes such as sparrow-beak milk jugs, pickle dishes or creamboats, although some rarities can even exceed £500 each. It is possible to concentrate on different types of decoration. You can collect a general theme such as armorial porcelain, and group together pieces from China and England over a long period, or you can specialise in a more specific subject, like overglaze transfer-printing on Worcester and Liverpool from the 1750s-1770s. English

£250-£500. Collecting a single shape is a good way to contrast the products of different makers, in this case Bristol, Vauxhall, Worcester, Bow, Lowestoft and Caughley. Rare creamboats without damage will cost more than £500, but plenty can still be found for less.

porcelain figures are surprisingly reasonable, and £400-£500 can buy an eighteenth century Bow or Derby figure in good condition. With more to spend you can purchase bigger and more decorative Dresden ornaments and impressive pairs of vases by the smaller makers made to show off. Meissen figures start at about £300 for small nineteenth century examples, but anything elaborate will cost much more. Berlin and Vienna are not nearly as expensive as Meissen and offer better value. Good figures by the minor factories like Sitzendorf and Plaue can be jolly decorative and should not be dismissed within this price range. Likewise, good examples of Japanese and Chinese decorative porcelain can be good value when well painted, especially matching pairs of Canton, Kutani and Imari vases. These

may not appeal to connoisseurs, but for display can be most impressive.

Collectors of eighteenth century porcelain may regard the twentieth century as totally lacking in taste, but there are many areas which do have a style of their own and sufficient quality to make them well worth collecting. Royal Crown Derby's Imari patterns are impressive when displayed together and the best pieces were made early this century. Royal Worcester at that time specialised in an apricot and ivory tinted porcelain known as 'Blush Ivory', and this is still plentiful although prices have risen steadily and it is hard to find bargains in a very popular market. Any worthwhile pieces of Worcester, Derby and Doulton by signed artists will cost you more than £500, but workmanship that is just as fine from smaller

£250-£500. Candle extinguishers make a fascinating collection. Most Royal Worcester examples sell for less than £500, with other makers generally cheaper. These depict Jenny Lind, the singer known as the 'Swedish Nightingale', and Mons. Reynard as a foxy lawyer.

£250-£500. A great many pairs of vases were exported from China and Japan around 1900 and the best provide good design and decoration today at an affordable price. This pair of Japanese vases is in the traditional Imari style.

More than £500. When collecting popular shapes it is important to aim for quality. These inkwells, tapersticks and baskets are by the best English makers of the 19th century and have obvious appeal.

factories will be far less expensive. I refer here to Staffordshire factories like Paragon, Aynsley and even Copeland, and Grainger and Hadley in Worcester. Expensive limited edition porcelain sculptures from the 1960s and '70s, especially the Royal Worcester horses, bird models and the Victorian Ladies, have proved disastrous investments over the years, but at their present prices these offer great opportunities at between £200-£400 for pieces that once sold for five times as much.

MORE THAN £500

It is incredible to think that at the upper end of the antique porcelain market dinner sets are actually bought to use, but this is a common occurrence, especially in the United States. Modern top-of-the-range dinner ware from the leading makers of the present day is so expensive that, considering the fine workmanship, nineteenth century Meissen, Coalport or Worcester services in rich patterns can still be better value. Even at prices in excess of £20,000, the antique sets certainly hold their resale value better.

It is worth looking at the modern cost of

making fine hand-decorated porcelain to appreciate the wares of the past. Factories with a long tradition of excellence often make today the same designs for which they have become famous. Meissen produces flower painted porcelain, Royal Crown Derby continues its popular Imari patterns, and Coalport makes flower-encrusted 'Coalbrookdale' vases. These all cost new far more than collectors have to pay for the equivalent eighteenth and nineteenth century pieces from the same factories.

It is hard to interpret the significance of this. Are antique pieces cheap or are new pieces overpriced?

Expensive pieces of antique porcelain are mostly bought to join collections of a similar type. Serious collectors used only to look at the eighteenth century, but nowadays, thank goodness, quality is a very important factor too. Thus the fine porcelain made after 1850 for exhibitions and wealthy connoisseurs is now given the credit it deserves.

Still, a very different sort of collector will enthuse over Meissen of the 1730s or Chelsea from the Red Anchor period as would delight in Berlin plaques, Sèvres style ormolu-

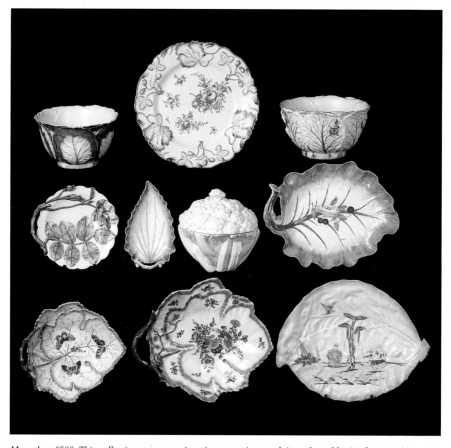

More than £500. This collection represents American taste in porcelain and would raise far more interest in New York than a selection of rare English blue and white. Decorative leaf shapes from Worcester, Chelsea and Longton Hall are as popular today as when they were made around 1760.

mounted vases and Royal Worcester vases by John Stinton. It is quite inappropriate to try to compare one collector with another, for they are as different as chalk and cheese.

In ten years Chinese Imperial Qianlong porcelain has increased in value many fold, while Export porcelain of the same period, once held in much higher regard, has held steady or even fallen in value. Analysts can look to the Hong Kong financial markets to explain differences, but no one can say a Chinese armorial tureen is in any way inferior to a Dragon Vase.

What is clear is that people collect for different reasons. In this book I have tried to explain the joys of early English blue and white, which many people find exciting. £10,000 will not buy many pieces of Limehouse or Lund's Bristol, but for a similar sum a collector could fill a large cabinet with Chinese blue and white porcelain of the same age. Some people will never understand the difference, and this does not really matter.

More than £500. Wedgwood 'Fairyland Lustre' is costly, but a group of pieces gathered together makes a magnificent display. Designed by Daisy Makeig-Jones, early 20th century.

What is important is that collectors willing to spend more than £500 on a single piece of porcelain have to appreciate its quality. Whether this is the quality of rarity, fine workmanship or simply classic design for decoration in the home is entirely up to the collector.

The display of leaf and vegetable shapes shown opposite is very much North American taste and consequently these pieces will sell for higher sums in New York. Germans pay far more for Meissen figures than Australians who prefer Royal Worcester and Doulton. Many collectors start off by admiring what their friends have and collect, and so the different taste of different countries is important. Everyone to their own, of course, but when high prices are concerned, the importance of fine condition and an accurate attribution cannot be stressed too strongly. Too many expensive mistakes are made by collectors who do not first gain a sufficient understanding of their chosen field.

CHAPTER 6

CHINA

The Chinese are rarely given credit by collectors of European porcelain for their enormous contribution to the art. They invented porcelain, of course, but, far more than this, every new shape, colour and design developed in China over the centuries has had a significant effect on the West. Most European potters aspired to copy Chinese porcelain as the valuable trade in Oriental goods spawned princely fortunes. Bitter rivalry between the first obsessive collectors even led their countries to the point of war in their anxiety to obtain the latest Chinese exports.

Porcelain was discovered in the seventh century, possibly by accident as some naturally occurring white clays contain both kaolin and felspar – the two crucial ingredients in the manufacture of porcelain. In the year 851 an Arab writer described Chinese pottery 'as fine as glass…the sparkle of water can be seen through it'. This was made at Jingdezhen which was to become the great porcelain

A Chinese saucer dish made for export and unusually painted with European figures, or at least a Chinese interpretation of how Dutchmen looked to them, c.1740.

manufacturing centre, with much of the wares exported through nearby Canton. The 'Silk Road' established in the Tang dynasty meant that ceramics from China were traded to other parts of Asia.

There is a major distinction between Chinese porcelain destined for export and pieces created for the Chinese themselves. Since the Song dynasty the finest was always reserved for the Emperor. Lesser quality Longquan celadon was exported to the Near East where the Ottoman sultans loved the rich glazes. During the fourteenth century the sultans lined the walls of the Topkapi palace with a magnificent array of Yuan dynasty dishes. This collection, along with fabulous Ming blue and white acquired during the fifteenth century, can still be seen in its original setting in Istanbul today.

Chinese blue and white used cobalt imported from Persia. During the Yuan dynasty supplies were plentiful and so boldly painted large dishes could be made; however, when the Mongols were overthrown to establish the Ming dynasty, foreign trade was curtailed. With cobalt in short supply, early Ming blue and white was painted with much greater care, using designs which were uncrowded and in total harmony with the plain shapes. Uneven grinding of the cobalt caused irregular dark specks in the blue painting; this so-called 'heaped and piled' effect was softened by the bubbled glaze which typifies early Ming.

Later in the fifteenth century, during the reign of Chenghua, many of the problems were overcome and some of the finest blue and white was made, typified by 'Palace' bowls clearly painted with trailing flowers below an ivory-tinted glaze. Chenghua porcelain sees the first use of enamel colours with a delicate blue outline filled in red, yellow and green in a palette called *doucai*. The most celebrated pieces are tiny bowls painted with chickens which epitomise all that is beautiful in Chinese

40

A magnificent large fencai *dish with the six character mark of the emperor Yongzheng. 20in. (51cm). Imperial* famille rose *is worlds apart from the* famille rose *made for export.*

porcelain. Many collectors dream of discovering a Chenghua chicken cup, for any authentic example would have a price tag in excess of a million pounds.

Colours were used more widely in the sixteenth century. Large jars painted with fish were made for the Emperor Zhengde in *wucai* or 'five-colours' which were not as subtle as *doucai*. Cheaper export wares were made during the reign of Wanli and, although often poorly potted, the designs are vivid and examples are still quite valuable. A Portuguese trading post at Macao in 1557 established a new export market in cheaper porcelain for South-East Asia, Japan and Europe. The so-called *Kraak* porcelain is typical of seventeenth century exports, painted in blue and white with Buddhist and Daoist emblems which meant nothing to wealthy European customers who wanted any porcelain to decorate the walls of their homes. The Dutch East India Company was founded in 1602 and sent special orders to China for porcelain in European taste. New colours were introduced. *Famille verte* developed from *wucai* during the reign of Kangxi early in the eighteenth century. A distinctive pink colour was brought from Europe by Jesuits and led to some of the most beautiful Imperial *famille rose* porcelain made within the Emperor's palace. Once perfected in the Yongzheng reign, *famille rose* was widely used for export porcelain sent in ever greater quantities to Europe, including specially ordered armorial services.

A Chinese teapot with dragons derived from fine Qing Imperial porcelain, but the seal mark of Guangxu dates this to the late 19th century. As a decorative export piece this is surprisingly inexpensive.   Sandon collection

The decoration of porcelain for export was in total contrast to the Imperial wares made in the Qing dynasty in Chinese taste. Early Ming patterns were copied in blue and white and *doucai*, sometimes with spurious Ming marks, but the smooth glassy glaze feels very different. The best pieces have honest Qing reign marks and today can be very valuable, having been reassessed in recent years. Values of Chinese export porcelain have changed little, while interest in Chinese taste porcelain has escalated. Such pieces were almost unknown in the West until the end of the nineteenth century. Travellers to China came back to Britain with Qing vases decorated with monochrome glazes known by descriptive names such as 'tea dust', 'robin's egg' or 'ox blood'. These were very different from the export porcelain made in enormous quantities in Jingdezhen and Canton – gaudy 'Rose Medallion' pattern teasets and crude copies of Kangxi blue and white vases.

Export designs reflect changes in European fashion, but generally Chinese taste porcelain is a continuing tradition. Ming patterns were very popular in the eighteenth and nineteenth centuries and Qing patterns are still popular today. If you visit a modern porcelain warehouse in Hong Kong you will be hard pushed to find any pattern that did not originate at least in the last century. To appreciate Chinese porcelain, collectors need to look with experience beyond the pattern to the spirit of the vessel itself and this should tell you when it was made.

A blanc de chine *figure of Buddha made at Dehua for the Chinese market and a typically Eastern piece, 9½in. (24cm), 18th or early 19th century.*

1. SONG AND YUAN PORCELAIN

Tang white wares and proto-porcelains are rarely offered for sale, but it is perfectly possible to collect Song porcelain. Twelfth century *Qingbai* porcelain was made at Jingdezhen, especially shallow conical bowls carved with scrolling flowers, with a bluish-green glaze that pools in the design. Many *Qingbai* bowls have recently become available in the West, apparently excavated from Song or Yuan sites, but these are coarse, both in body and design, compared with the finer pieces from Jingdezhen. Marco Polo described 'inexpensive bowls the colour of azure' and he may have seen these more simple productions which are still reasonably priced today. Conical bowls with carved decoration were also made at Ding Zhou in the north, but these are whiter with a most attractive ivory-tinted glaze. *Ding* porcelain was brittle and the unglazed rims of bowls were edged with a copper band for protection.

Celadon developed differently in the northern and southern centres during the Song and Yuan dynasties. *Yaozhou* or Northern Celadon is olive-green in colour with a grey body and strong carved shapes, while *Longquan* from the south is whiter with a smooth blue-green glaze over very subtle carving. Yuan celadon was exported in quantity to the Near East but most Celadon found in Europe is of later Ming date. Blue painting was introduced in the Yuan dynasty and some simple vessels and provincial pieces are surprisingly affordable today considering their age. These can be exciting, but they hardly begin to compare with fine Yuan blue and white. Large dishes with barbed rims were painted with fish among swirling water or ducks beside reeds, framed with pretty flower borders. These pieces may not be as fine technically as later Ming wares, but the combination of powerful designs and somewhat coarse potting gives Yuan blue and white an excitement all of its own.

Further reading
Margaret Medley: *The Art of the Chinese Potter,* 1981

A Qingbai *bowl carved with typical scrolls and clouds, from the Southern Song dynasty, 8½in. (22cm), 13th century.* Sandon collection

Two Longquan celadon circular dishes datable to the Ming dynasty, probably sixteenth century. The incised lotus design (right) is typically subtle, 13in. and 13¼in. (33 and 34cm).

2. MING PORCELAIN

The name Ming is synonymous with value in the art world, and some Ming vases have changed hands for enormous sums. It must be remembered, though, that the Ming dynasty lasted 275 years and many pieces of porcelain made during the Ming dynasty are actually worth very little. Simple pots and jarlets for the South-east Asian market were crude and cheap, products of provincial kilns worlds apart from the wonderful Imperial kilns at Jingdezhen. The Ming Emperors took particular interest in porcelain, often supervising the designs themselves and permitting the fine wares to be marked with their names. Such close dating greatly assists the study of Chinese porcelain as comparisons can be made of the same shape and design produced during different reigns.

Early Ming blue and white, from the reigns of Yongle and Xuande, is the most exciting. Potters created new shapes and patterns while struggling to overcome difficulties with a cloudy glaze and uneven cobalt blue that burnt in patches causing the effect known as 'heaping and piling'. By the fifteenth century reign of Chenghua the blue was perfectly controlled, however, giving the painting a unique delicacy and freedom. Figure subjects tell stories and formal flower designs take on great meaning. Enamelling was introduced and in the *doucai* palette 'contrasting' colours appear like jewels set into delicate underglaze blue drawings in a style reminiscent of traditional Chinese painting. Chenghua porcelain comes close to perfection, so understandably was followed by decline during the sixteenth century. The vivid palette of *wucai* was used to great effect in the reign of Zhengde on vessels painted with fish, although other pieces with the same mixture of five colours made for the Near-eastern market can seem crude and are often poorly potted.

Late Ming porcelain from the reign of Wanli can be fine in its own way but does not stand comparison with the products of two centuries earlier. Most was aimed at a different and much less discerning market in Japan, Portugal, and South-East Asia. *Kraak* porcelain, named after ships called carracks that traded from the Portuguese base at Macao, ranges greatly in quality. Some dishes are truly magnificent and, considering this is Ming after all, some *Kraak* porcelain is not particularly expensive.

A Jiajing polychrome jar of a type popular with the Ottoman Turks. The painting can seem coarse, but in the sixteenth century such pieces were greatly prized.

Further reading

Soames Jenyns: *Ming Pottery and Porcelain,* 1953

Duncan Macintosh: *Chinese Blue and White,* revised ACC, 1994

Margaret Medley: *The Art of the Chinese Potter,* 1981

---

3. QING IMPERIAL PORCELAIN

Generations of collectors have admired Chinese export porcelain, while porcelain made in the Chinese taste had been largely ignored in the West. Over the past two decades this situation has been transformed. Qing Imperial porcelain is now appreciated for the art that it represents. Imperial porcelain is built around tradition. When the Manchu emperors came to power in 1644 and brought peace to the country, they looked back to the 'Golden Age' of Chinese art. The new emperors wanted to show that they were the legitimate successors of the great Ming rulers by proving that the qualities inherent in Yongle, Xuande and Chenghua porcelain were

A copy of a Ming jar made for the Emperor Qianlong in the 18th century. The accidental effect of 'heaping and piling', seen on early Ming pieces, has been copied with careful brushwork. It is important that this vase bears the reign mark of Qianlong rather than a copy of an earlier Ming mark.

not lost to them. They set the Imperial kilns the task of copying and equalling classic Ming porcelain kept in the palace. The kilns at Jingdezhen had changed little, although the Qing blue and white painters now had to imitate the old 'heaped and piled' effect caused in the fifteenth century by uneven cobalt particles. Qing copies often bear the original Ming marks and imitate the designs and glaze very closely. As a result only an experienced specialist can distinguish the best eighteenth century copies from genuine Ming, especially the copies of Chenghua *doucai.*

The Qing rulers also desired new porcelain designs by which their own reigns would be remembered. Jesuit priests helped the Chinese develop a pink enamel they had brought from Europe. Imperial *famille rose* porcelain called *yuzhi,* enamelled in the palace itself during the Kangxi reign, is of exceptional rarity and beauty. There is an enormous difference

This Qianlong moon vase is painted with an Imperial dragon in underglaze red and blue, a rare combination which was difficult to control, even in the Imperial kilns at Jingdezhen.

An ancient Chinese metal shape, well suited to this single colour turquoise glaze, 14½in. (37cm), 18th century.

between Yongzheng and Qianlong *famille rose* made in quantity for export and the truly special pieces made for the Emperor's court. These include the so-called *Guyue Xuan*, vases painted with traditional Chinese flowering rocks and birds with a delicacy all of their own. These have always been sought after, although until recently nineteenth century Imperial porcelain had been neglected. Today fine Jiaqing and Daoguang porcelain fetches large sums, and even Guangxu pieces made at the turn of this century can be valuable if the quality is there and they bear the honest mark of the period in which they were made.

Further reading

M. Beurdeley and G. Raindre: *Qing Porcelain: Famille Verte and Famille Rose*, 1987

R. Kerr: *Chinese Ceramics: Porcelain of the Qing Dynasty*, 1986

S. Kwan: *Imperial Porcelain of the Late Qing*, 1983

4. MONOCHROMES AND OTHER GLAZES

As well as imitating Ming painted pieces, the Qing potters attempted exact copies of dramatic Song and Yuan glaze effects such as the *Kuan* ware with its thick crackled glaze, and various celadons. Some ancient glazes had evolved over centuries and careful experimentation was necessary to reproduce exactly effects such as 'tea dust' which has the appearance of ancient bronze. Qing copies of Ming bowls and dishes are as delicate as the originals with lightly incised dragons beneath the richest shade of yellow or green.

While working to perfect their copies, chemists at the Imperial kilns invented new glaze colours as fine as any from the past.

A group of Kangxi porcelain in the distinctive palette of famille verte. *Sets of vases such as these were popular exports to Europe. The bowl is unusual and more in Chinese taste with rare added gilding.*

'Peach bloom' was created from a copper-based glaze that changed in tone depending on the firing. The Chinese attempted a perfectly even form of the glaze, but most examples developed irregular patches of grey or green which were seen not as faults but as magical strengths. Peach bloom was mostly used on small items for scholars, especially water-pots and brushwashers. 'Robin's egg' glaze is a brilliant turquoise softened by streaks of purple with a most appealing feel to the surface.

Chinese monochromes need to be held to appreciate their beauty, and in some cases just to tell they are porcelain at all, for a rich coral glaze developed in the reign of Qianlong reproduced exactly the appearance of lacquer. Most of the famous glazes continued throughout later Qing reigns and dating pieces requires a specialist knowledge and a well-tuned eye. Many glazes are still made today, Peach bloom in particular, but while new pieces can be attractive, they lack the magic achieved in the eighteenth century.

Further reading

Margaret Medley: *The Art of the Chinese Potter,* 1981

5. FAMILLE VERTE

A new range of colours was developed during the Kangxi reign, primarily for use on porcelain for export. It followed on from the *wucai* or five-colour palette by replacing the underglaze blue with an overglaze blue enamel. As the illustration shows, the main colours are a translucent green and a bright red. Black was used to outline the design which was filled in with coloured washes of blue, yellow and a very pale aubergine-purple. Gold was used sparingly on special pieces.

The enamels were applied thickly and in some cases pooled unevenly. To disguise the effect of this, black dots or other fine patterns were often painted on top of the green and yellow, especially in the borders. When applied thickly the enamels can be unstable and may

A Chinese famille rose *tureen and stand from the Qianlong period with typical pink diaper panels and border, the stand 14½in. (37cm) long, c.1775.*

crack or even flake off. *Famille verte* was given its name in the nineteenth century when a great many copies were made, especially vases bearing Kangxi marks. Original pieces, made from about 1695 until 1730, are often marked with a precious symbol within concentric lines in underglaze blue. The glaze is often quite pitted and tends to flake off in parts around the rim. Designs are mostly of an oriental nature, although a range of special armorial dishes was made for customers in Holland and England. The most sought after pieces use black enamel as a solid background, the so-called *famille noir* which again was much copied. Once *famille rose* was perfected at the end of the Kangxi period, *famille verte* was completely replaced.

Further reading

Geoffrey Godden: *Oriental Export Market Porcelain,* 1979

6. FAMILLE ROSE

It is difficult to discuss *famille rose* in a general way as the distinctive pink-coloured enamel after which it is named has been used for nearly three centuries. The colour was brought from Europe early in the eighteenth century and Jesuit priests are believed to have helped the Chinese to develop it within the Emperor's palace. *Famille rose* is far more than a single new colour, however. It was really a new method of mixing ceramic colours, allowing different tones to be blended and shaded. The bright rose pink is usually prominent in the design, but not always. The earliest export pieces using the pink colour date from about 1730 and are of the same clumsy nature as much of the *famille verte.*

During the reign of Yongzheng, however, the quality of enamelled porcelain improved significantly and some of the finest pieces were

Two export mugs based on the shape of European creamware originals. The decoration comprises so-called 'Mandarin' figures and flowers possibly copied from Meissen, 6in. and 6¼in. (15cm. and 16cm), c.1770-80.

made, especially teawares of eggshell thinness. These were now enamelled in Canton in special factories rather than at the kiln site in Jingdezhen. Apart from the special orders and armorial pieces discussed separately, most of the patterns painted in *famille rose* are traditionally Chinese. Flowers and bird subjects are never symmetrical and instead spread across the shapes with an elegant sense of movement. Peonies were popular as these show the delicate shaded pink colour to best advantage. Narrative figure subjects told stories which would have meant nothing to the Europeans, but they were entranced by the charm of the little Chinese people painted on their teasets and tankards. The elegant patterns favoured by the Europeans were replaced early in the nineteenth century by a more heavily decorated style suited to the taste of new customers in the Middle East.

Eighteenth century *famille rose* plates, teapots and mugs are plentiful today and very attractive collections can be formed on a modest budget. Condition is important, however, as even slight damage greatly reduces the value.

Further reading

Geoffrey Godden: *Oriental Export Market Porcelain,* 1979

David Howard and John Ayres: *China for the West,* 1978

7. BLUE AND WHITE FOR EXPORT

The size of the trade in Chinese blue and white porcelain was graphically shown in 1985 when Captain Hatcher recovered the cargo of the Dutch East Indiaman *Geldermalsen* which foundered on its journey from Canton in 1752. On board were nearly a quarter of a million pieces of Chinese porcelain, mostly blue and white tea and dinner sets intended for homes across Europe. These were not special orders and the designs were traditional Chinese flowers, landscapes and river scenes. Customers in the West were delighted with the strength and durability of this porcelain and it found a ready market. The bulk export of blue and white began early in the seventeenth century when *Kraak* porcelain dishes and bowls were shipped to Portugal and on to Holland and the

A very large blue and white punchbowl with a typical Chinese subject which appealed greatly to European customers, 21½in. (54.5cm).

rest of Europe. Cheaper wares, thick and with clumsy painting, were sent to Japan, India and all parts of Southern Asia. Shipments to Europe were concluded early in the nineteenth century although the Chinese still supplied America.

Later in the nineteenth century a new trade developed sending copies of Kangxi dishes and vases to the West for use as ornaments. The result of this vast trade is an abundant supply of Chinese blue and white porcelain available to collectors today. Considering the age and general high quality, Qianlong export porcelain is not expensive. Plates rarely exceed £50 or £70 and cups or teabowls are often less than £10. Large dishes are more expensive and rarities can be highly priced, especially pretty shapes like salts. Earlier Kangxi export porcelain was painted with greater care and inevitably will cost more, but there is still plenty of opportunity for a collector. Early vases are scarce but late copies are plentiful and although the quality can be disappointing, good examples make nice decoration.

Further reading

Geoffrey Godden: *Oriental Export Market Porcelain,* 1979

Duncan Macintosh: *Chinese Blue and White Porcelain,* revised ACC, 1994

Colin Sheaf and R. Kilburn: *The Hatcher Porcelain Cargoes,* 1988

9. ARMORIAL DESIGNS AND SPECIAL ORDERS

The captain and the crew of ships trading with China were permitted to engage in their own 'private trade' in luxury goods, aside from the bulk cargoes of blue and white and *famille rose* table-sets. A director of the East India Company known as a 'super-cargo' usually travelled with the ship and took special orders with him to Canton. While the ship was in port, patterns would be enamelled to exclusive European designs. Orders placed for full armorial dinner services would be ready for collection when the

A group of items from a Yongzheng service, each piece bearing the arms of Skinner. The shapes follow European prototypes and one of the jugs has original European silver mounts. The dishes 19in. (48.5cm), c.1730.

ship returned the following year. Wealthy families chose their patterns from books of designs in London and sent a drawing of their coat of arms to be faithfully copied by the Chinese. High prices were charged but even so demand was considerable. The sets were too costly to use every day and were mostly kept for display in the home. Consequently armorial porcelain was well looked after and a high proportion of the sets made still survive. With the emphasis these days on Chinese taste porcelain, the value of the best Export china has stayed level. Now is a good time to consider building a collection of Chinese Export and there is enormous variety available in the special designs made for European customers.

Aside from the heraldic patterns, customers sent paintings of their houses and popular prints to be painted on to Chinese porcelain. Some pieces copied European engravings in black line drawings known as *encre de chine* or *grisaille,* but most of the special orders were executed in full *famille rose* colours. Specimens of Meissen and other European porcelain were copied faithfully by the Chinese, including factory marks that can cause much confusion. All manner of household objects were also sent to China to be copied, ranging from silver sauceboats and candlesticks to glass perfume bottles and wooden snuff boxes. Objects like these are rare and desirable in Chinese porcelain and will always be expensive.

Further reading

Geoffrey Godden: *Oriental Export Market Porcelain,* 1979

David Howard and John Ayres: *China for the West,* 1978

David Howard: *Chinese Armorial Porcelain,* 1974

Dr. C.J.A. Jorg: *Chinese Export Porcelain from the Royal Museums of Art and History in Brussels,* 1989

A Chinese mug with a popular blue and white design coloured in the Imari style for export to Europe, Qianlong, c.1760.

9. CHINESE IMARI

This contradictory term is used to describe Chinese porcelain made in the style of Japanese Imari. There was a large market in Europe for Japanese porcelain, but from about 1730 the Japanese severely restricted all trade with the West. The Chinese saw a great opportunity and copied the patterns and colours that had formerly been shipped from Imari. Patterns in underglaze blue, overglaze red, orange and gold were painted on to dinnerwares, teasets and a great many mugs. The Chinese plates were much thinner than the Japanese Imari ones had been, and the blue was far less intense. It is therefore not difficult to distinguish Chinese Imari from earlier Japanese, especially as most of the patterns are Chinese in origin, and it is only the colouring that was borrowed from Japan.

Further reading
Oriental Ceramic Society: *Porcelain For Palaces,* exhibition catalogue, 1990

10. CANTON AND ROSE MEDALLION

European porcelain took away custom previously enjoyed by the Chinese and in the nineteenth century Cantonese traders searched for new markets. Certain patterns had been popular with customers in India and the Middle East and from about 1820 the enamellers concentrated on this distinctive style. The so-called 'Canton' style was exported initially to Persia but subsequently to America and Europe as well. The colourful patterns found a ready market in the United States where they became known as 'Rose Medallion', for they featured panels or medallions of *famille rose* enamelling. These were the successors of the 'Mandarin' style of rich figure decoration made

The shapes of this Canton teaset, with handled cups and a milk jug, show it was made for export to Europe or America. The quality is poor, but such colourful wares enjoyed enormous popularity. 19th century.

during the eighteenth century. Naturally these wares were aimed at a range of new markets and came in different levels of quality to suit different pockets.

Some nineteenth century Canton porcelain can be very fine, especially earlier examples from the Jiaqing and Daoguang reigns up until 1850. The finest bowls and saucer dishes have additional panels of painted Persian script which enable a few examples to be dated. Mostly, however, the same shapes continued, even well into the twentieth century, and specimens can be extremely difficult to date. Some examples can be scruffy and have little real merit to them, especially teasets marked 'China' or 'Made in China', marks put on after 1891. On the other hand, impressive pairs of vases, in an enormous range of sizes, are highly decorative and understandably popular, especially with collectors in today's Middle East. A range of plates and dessert dishes was made for Europe, often painted with insects and flowers on a celadon-glazed ground. Thin examples can be very pleasing, but many are crude and thick and deserve to be inexpensive.

Further reading

Herbert, Peter and Nancy Schiffer: *Chinese Export Porcelain: Standard Patterns and Forms, 1780-1880,* U.S.A., 1975

---

11. BLANC DE CHINE

Blanc de Chine is a nineteenth century term used by collectors to refer to the white glazed porcelain made at Dehua in Fujian province. It is usual for such wares to be described as Dehua today, but the alternative French name is very well established. The creamy white porcelain was exported through Amoy rather than Canton and shapes were very much in the Chinese taste. Figures of Buddha and the Goddess Guanyin, lion joss-stick holders and porcelain copies of rhino horn libation cups were designed to sit in Eastern shrines. They were considered curiosities when they arrived in Europe and, unsure of their market, china dealers in London sold the Guanyin figures as

A rare group of European figures which was imported along with the Buddhas and Guanyins. In 1703 'Dutch Families' sold for up to 3 shillings each in London. 6¼in. (16cm) high.

'Sancta Marias', even though they had no obvious Christian attributes. Dehua ornaments were imported in quantity for about twenty years between 1690 and about 1710, and were very inexpensive. A range of amusing models of Dutchmen was made, but mostly the models were bought as Chinese curiosities. They must have been keenly collected, for some of the bowls and cups were mounted in silver in Europe. Once importation had ceased they were copied in Meissen porcelain in the 1720s and in English porcelain thirty years later. Ironically these European forgeries are today worth a great deal more than the Dehua originals. There is simply no comparison between the inexpensive export figures and wonderful *Blanc de Chine* sculptures subsequently made at Dehua for the Chinese themselves (see page 43). Many of the white Dehua beakers and mugs were enamelled with crude colouring in Holland and England, causing much confusion over their origin.

Further reading

P.J. Donnelly: *Blanc de Chine,* 1969
Geoffrey Godden: *Oriental Export Market Porcelain,* 1979

CHAPTER 7

JAPAN

The traditional arts of Japan have always held a great fascination for European collectors. Porcelain is not an ancient craft as in China, for it was only introduced to Japan in the seventeenth century. Early specimens of blue and white *shoki- Imari,* made for The Tea Ceremony, can appear clumsy to Western eyes, rather like the *ko-sometsuke* ware made in China for the Japanese market. Production was based around Arita and shipped through the port of Imari, two names associated with export porcelain painted just in blue or in the distinctive red, blue and gold palette. Japan mistrusted foreigners, but a limited trade with Holland allowed impressive Imari vases and dishes to reach wealthy European homes.

A very different porcelain was made for the Japanese themselves. Nabeshima is as mysterious and exciting as it is expensive today, a work of art in every sense. A very distinctive palette of enamel colours is associated with the Kakiemon dynasty of potters. In contrast to vulgar Imari, Kakiemon is very restrained, and suited the much more discerning Chinese market. British ships were forbidden to trade with Japan and so the Chinese sold Kakiemon on to British merchants for a profit. Although expensive, Japanese porcelain was treasured in Europe and led to many imitations, especially from the Chinese who copied Imari colours.

The Japanese chose not to compete with the Chinese and from the 1740s began a century of self-imposed isolation. A limited export trade was re-established with America in the 1850s, and gradually other countries including Britain explored this exciting new market. The Japanese display at the 1867 Paris Exhibition caused a sensation. There is much more to nineteenth century Japanese porcelain than the clumsy copies of old Imari. The beautiful porcelain in Japanese taste, made at Hirado and by the Fukagawa and Makuzu Kozan factories, was refreshingly different and attracted the eye of European connoisseurs. Early twentieth century exports reached staggering proportions. Imari plates and dishes, Kutani vases with rich red and gold designs, and Noritake eggshell teasets were sold in every china shop in Europe and America. Most were inexpensive and provided customers with cheap decoration. The best pieces, however, were superbly potted and represent the finest Japanese crafts-manship.

An Arita Ko-Imari *ovoid jar from the* Edo *period, mid-17th century. Although influenced by Chinese porcelain, the design and colouring are quite different, 15in. (38cm).*

A Kakiemon incense-burner and cover, c.1700, of a metal form, a mythical karashishi *forming the finial, 5in. (12.5cm) high.*

1. KAKIEMON

Although strictly associated with only a single family of potters, descendants of Sakaida Kakiemon, the name Kakiemon is more widely used to describe a style of decoration made at Arita from about 1670 until the early eighteenth century. Most appears to have been made in a single kiln where blue and white porcelain was also made, but it is for a distinctive palette of enamel colours that Kakiemon is universally famed. The beautiful white body, called *nigoshide* or 'milky white', is superior to most other Japanese porcelain and sets off the semi-translucent enamels. The patterns are usually very restrained, leaving much of the white porcelain as a bright background. Designs are mostly floral, usually clear red flowers on sharp stems of blue and green leaves sometimes heightened in gold. Birds are often included as well as a curious menagerie of dragons and *kylin* derived from Chinese sources, for Kakiemon found a ready market in China. Rare figure subjects include the Chinese boy Sima

Qian who threw stones to break a large pottery jar and prevent a friend drowning inside. This Song dynasty story was interpreted by Japanese painters and the appealing design was later copied at Meissen and at Chelsea. It became known in eighteenth century England as the 'Hob-in-the-Well' pattern. Kakiemon had been keenly collected in England from as early as the 1670s. What little was available came by way of China. Production in Japan ceased during the 1730s and copies were subsequently made throughout Europe.

A fascinating collection can be formed of Kakiemon designs made at different factories, although many pieces are very expensive today.

Further reading

John Ayres, Oliver Impey and John Mallet: *Porcelain for Palaces, The Fashion for Japan in Europe,* 1990

Soame Jenyns: *Japanese Porcelain,* 1965

Gordon Lang: *The Wrestling Boys,* catalogue of an exhibition of Japanese porcelain in the collection at Burleigh House, 1983

A large Imari baluster vase unusually painted with open screens. Standing 35½in. (90cm) high, this would have looked magnificent in a grand European home or palace in 1700.

2. IMARI

The port of Imari lies close to the porcelain producing region of Arita. Few Europeans were permitted access to Japan and instead they bought Japanese porcelain from Chinese trading posts. Confused about its origin, early Europeans believed a distinctive kind of Japanese porcelain had been made at Imari. The same kilns at Arita made both blue and white and enamelled porcelain. The name Imari was widely used to refer to porcelain which combined underglaze blue and overglaze red and gold, a combination which attracted Dutch traders in particular. Additional colours such as green, yellow and purple were sometimes included, and some pieces do not use any underglaze blue at all.

While it is debatable whether all enamelled Arita should be called Imari, there is no denying the popularity this distinctive porcelain has enjoyed over the years. Sets of vases and circular dishes, often of large size, decorated the walls of European homes as a welcome change from plain blue and white Chinese exports. When Japan suspended overseas trade around 1740, traders looked to China to replace the popular Japanese designs. Great quantities of 'Chinese Imari' came to Europe in the eighteenth century and Imari patterns were copied by many European porcelain factories. In Regency England old Japanese Imari, one hundred years old, was highly valued. Porcelain makers realised the potential and the English 'Japan' style became the height of fashion with Derby as the leader. When the Japanese re-established an export trade later in the nineteenth century, Imari patterns were made as if there had been no interruption. Exact copies of seventeenth and early eighteenth century patterns were made in enormous quantity. Fortunately it is not difficult to learn to tell early Japanese Imari from late. At both periods the quality varies greatly and is an

An Arita jug made in the same kilns as the more colourful Imari wares and produced for the Dutch market at the end of the 17th century. The inspiration is Chinese, however.

important criteria in determining value. Some early twentieth century pieces are very crude and clumsy, but the best, made at factories such as Fukagawa, are technically far superior to anything from the early days of Imari.

Further reading

John Ayres, Oliver Impey and John Mallet: *Porcelain for Palaces, The Fashion for Japan in Europe,* 1990

Geoffrey Godden: *Oriental Export Market Porcelain,* 1979

Soame Jenyns: *Japanese Porcelain,* 1965

An eccentric but beautifully made teapot by Makuzu Kozan in the form of a pagoda, 6½in. (17cm). Such pieces appealed to Chinese customers as well as Europeans.

3. NABESHIMA WARES

Made for the Lords of Nabeshima for their private use and for presentation to Shoguns and other feudal lords, this is really the Japanese equivalent of Chinese Imperial porcelain. Indeed, some of the decoration mirrors the *doucai* of early Qing. Carefully drawn outlines in underglaze blue are filled-in in contrasting enamel colours on a creamy porcelain or celadon background. Other Nabeshima is just in blue and white. Small circular dishes and pretty cups are notable for their smooth finish and for the asymmetry of the designs. Examples from the finest period early in the eighteenth century are extremely valuable and rarely seen outside Japan. Pieces continued to be made in the nineteenth century, however, and also detailed copies of early Nabeshima porcelain were made. It can take an experienced eye to distinguish these from the priceless originals.

Further reading
Soame Jenyns: *Japanese Porcelain,* 1965

4. HIRADO, FUKAGAWA AND MAKUZU KOZAN

During the period of self-imposed isolation, Japanese porcelain continued to be made for the home market totally different in taste from the wares previously exported to China and the West. The inspiration came partly from early Nabeshima pieces which were precisely copied, and in addition potters looked to other

It is easy to imagine an ivory dog of Fo cast in porcelain to make this delicate Hirado model, 4in. (10cm), late 19th century.

traditional Japanese crafts such as ivory carving and woodblock printing.

Many of these fine nineteenth century Japanese porcelains have an individual quality far removed from any factory made objects. Indeed, the 'factories' of Hirado and Makuzu Kozan were really a series of individual kilns. Hirado porcelain is very white and can be finely modelled. Decoration in bright underglaze blue is often incredibly detailed, and remarkable piercing or reticulation was carried out with a precision to equal the skills of ivory workers. The colours used by Eizaiemon Fukagawa and his followers resemble Arita export porcelain, but the designs are in a different dimension, precisely drawn and carefully shaded with the subtlety of Japanese screen painting. The value of fine Makuzu Kozan porcelain has risen dramatically, as col-

lectors in Europe as well as in Japan have realised the skill and often breathtaking beauty fused into every piece. Other signed artists, such as Seifu Yohei III are also greatly in demand, particularly in Japan. Although apparently in Japanese taste, some of the most individual potters were based in Yokohama to take advantage of the port's significance in the export market. Examples of fine Art Porcelain were bought by European connoisseurs travelling in Japan and often formed gifts to foreign diplomats. Fine pieces can be found in England, the United States and Australia and deserve the high prices they now command.

Further reading

Kathleen Emerson Dell: *Bridging East and West: Japanese Ceramics from the Kozan Studio,* Exhibition catalogue, 1995

An imposing scale (35½in., 90cm) and exceptional painting lifts this Kutani jar way above most other pieces of Japanese export porcelain. A costly production which would be highly valued today.

5. KUTANI

A distinctive palette of flame red or orange with black details and gilding is associated with the name of Kutani although its origin is confused. Porcelain painted in this style was also made in kilns at Arita, Noritake and Kyoto and identical shapes and patterns occur in crackle-glazed earthenware. Pairs of vases, teasets, little bottles for Sake and big dishes for display, all varied enormously in quality to suit different customers.

Liberty's in London sold these with the exotic names of 'Kaga Ware' and 'Kutani' and in 1920 a typical pair of 10 inch high vases retailed for 11 shillings. Some figure painting, and especially bird decoration, was of a very high standard and good Kutani vases are deservedly expensive, especially when of large size.

Further reading

Irene Stitt: *Japanese Ceramics of the Last 100 Years,* New York, 1974

Appropriately named, this Noritake 'eggshell' teaset of c.1910 is intricately painted in an attractive Eastern style. Fine workmanship for just a few pounds a piece today.

6. NORITAKE

The ubiquitous Japanese eggshell tea and coffee services have become objects of derision in the antiques trade because of the sheer quantities that exist. Hardly a family in Europe or America did not own at least one Japanese set, for they were extremely cheap, very decorative and at the same time mysterious, with geisha girls staring out from the bottom of each cup when held up to the light. Between 1900 and 1940 many millions of pieces were exported from Japan and sold in every High Street. No European factory could make a teaset so cheaply, and at times Noritake eggshell threatened the very livelihood of Stoke-on-Trent. Samurai warriors or views of Mount Fuji were crudely painted on the inexpensive sets and finely painted on the best. Cheap and nasty examples have virtually no merit, but the costly

sets in their day were very beautifully painted in the Japanese taste and in terms of workmanship deserve serious recognition.

The Japanese porcelain industry concentrated on mass exports and copied anything that would sell in the West. Chinese dragons, Arabian dessert scenes, Alpine cottages and bowls of English fruit were repeatedly painted in the vast factories at Noritake. Vases, fruit sets and powder bowls copied the latest styles from Royal Worcester, Dresden or Vienna. Such ornaments were never meant to be works of art, and therefore have been neglected by most porcelain enthusiasts. Very decorative pieces are only now starting to be appreciated in England, although for some time pieces marked 'Nippon China' have been collectable in the United States. A wide variety of marks was used, usually printed in green with words in English.

ITALY

Marked with the crowned N of Naples and popularly known as Capodimonte, this casket is typical of the confusion that is late Italian porcelain. Probably made by Ginori, early 20th century.

Italy led Europe in fine pottery making in the sixteenth century with colourful maiolica, and so it is hardly surprising porcelain was first made in Florence a century before any other European translucent porcelain. Produced under the patronage of the Grand Duke Francesco I de Medici between 1575 and 1587, Medici porcelain combined East and West, uniting the freshness of early Ming blue and white with the formal splendour of the Italian Renaissance. The Duke hoped for vast wealth but was fraught by heavy kiln failures and customers who preferred Italian maiolica or real Chinese porcelain brought back by trade to Venice. Two pieces of Medici porcelain sold in recent years for more than one million pounds each. It truly deserves to be expensive, and is simply not available to private collectors.

Beautiful pottery continued to be made, but Italy had to wait until others had discovered the secret before any other porcelain was made. C.C. Hunger learnt the secret processes working at Meissen and Vienna, and in Venice his new backer, Francesco Vezzi, produced a creamy hard paste porcelain for about fifteen years from 1720. Vezzi porcelain, often bearing the name mark of Venezia, lacked the whiteness of Meissen and its shapes and decoration were often primitive. It does have a natural excitement, however, not seen in more sophisticated porcelain. A very individual Italian soft paste porcelain was made at Capodimonte for Charles III, King of Naples from 1743 until about 1759, and then the works were moved to Buen Retiro in Spain and fell into decline. Delicate modelling and subtle painting gives Capodimonte a unique beauty and a legendary name that was much abused in later centuries.

The most successful Italian porcelain was made by the Ginori family in their factory at

A sculptural quality is inherent in all Doccia figures, coupled with a distinctive style of colouring which is unique to Italy. This group dates from 1755-65.

Coarse, but early with an excitement of its own, this Vezzi cup and saucer was probably inspired by Chinese blanc de chine, *c.1730.*

Doccia near Florence from about 1735 until the late nineteenth century. Doccia survived in spite of competition from a royal factory set up at Naples by King Ferdinand IV. Naples porcelain was mostly in neo-classical taste, inspired by excavations at Pompeii and notable for high quality modelling and decoration.

Several other small factories made porcelain in Italy in the eighteenth century, including Cozzi's works in Venice which operated from 1764 until about 1812, making hard paste with a thick, creamy iridescent glaze. Cozzi porcelain is often marked with an anchor in red causing confusion with Chelsea, but the Cozzi anchor is very large and easily distinguished from the neat and tiny Chelsea mark. Other Italian marks – the fleur-de-lis of Capodimonte and the crowned N of Naples – were much imitated late in the nineteenth century, principally on pieces made in the style of Doccia. The mixed-up later Italian style was generically termed Capodimonte by Victorian collectors and the name has stuck, used for anything bearing a crowned N mark or vaguely in Italian style. Such pieces can be decorative, but generally lack any originality.

1. VEZZI

The first factory to make true porcelain in Italy was established by Francesco Vezzi using the skills of an itinerant ceramicist, Christoph Conrad Hunger, who arrived in Venice in 1720. Vezzi hoped to produce a fine porcelain to rival that of Meissen, and used kaolin smuggled in from Germany, but his glaze was generally creamy-grey instead of pure white and the wares were rarely as well potted as the German products of similar date. Teapots can be delightfully misshapen and have their own charm, mostly lacking the sophistication of Meissen which they emulated. Gilding was rarely used and instead a combination of red and green enamels are often seen together in sparse floral decorations which appear clumsy. The factory closed in 1727. Many pieces were clearly marked with the name Venezia, usually shortened to Vena. Vezzi porcelain is exciting because of its early date and is always expensive.

Further reading
Arthur Lane: *Italian Porcelain,* 1964
Francesco Stazzi: *Italian Porcelain,* 1967

Although inspired by Meissen, the grey glaze and flamboyant painting gives this mid-18th century Doccia plate a very different appearance.

2. DOCCIA

Much confusion surrounds the Ginori factory at Doccia, near Florence, mostly due to the very different appearance of the glaze used there at various times. The Marquis Carlo Ginori founded the factory in the mid-1730s, engaging a decorator from Vienna, but progress was slow and little porcelain appears to have been made at Doccia until about ten years had passed. The early glaze was thick and can be very grey, a feature shared by much Italian porcelain. Attempts to improve the glaze included adding tin oxide to the mixture resulting in a unique porcelain with the appearance of faïence.

At its best Doccia porcelain is sculptural, using dramatic shapes often left in the white. Powerful figures of saints were made, some of large size although these were rather prone to firing cracks. To compensate for the greyness of the glaze, very strong enamel colours were

A coffee jug in old Naples style probably made by the Ginori family late in the 19th century, well past the glory days of Doccia.

used, applied with great care and often using a stipple painting technique to add subtlety, particularly to the faces and hands of the figures. Porcelain tablewares modelled with figures in low relief were a speciality of the factory, left in white glazed porcelain or brightly coloured. These can date from the eighteenth century, but most surviving examples are much later.

The Ginori family continued to make porcelain until the 1890s and specialised in cups and saucers with figures in relief, as well as plaques and caskets. Occasionally these were marked with a star in red or gold, a mark associated with old Doccia, and sometimes the Ginori name was impressed. Most late Ginori porcelain was marked, however, with a copy of the crowned N of Naples in underglaze blue, for the Ginori factory had purchased what was left of the failed Naples works and claimed to be its legitimate successor. Victorian collectors thought these copied Capodimonte porcelain and the

name of Capodimonte is inextricably mixed up with late copies of Doccia and porcelain bearing the mark of a letter N and a crown.

Further reading
Geoffrey Godden: *Guide to European Porcelain*, 1993
Arthur Lane: *Italian Porcelain*, 1964

---

3. CAPODIMONTE

Genuine Capodimonte (or Capo di Monte) is justly regarded to be amongst the most beautiful porcelain ever made, although the name has become debased by endless later copies. Under the patronage of Charles III of Bourbon, the King of Naples, porcelain was made at Capodimonte for only sixteen or so years, from 1743 until about 1759 when the works were moved to Buen Retiro in Spain.

The porcelain was a creamy soft paste that was ideally suited to the modelling of Giuseppe Gricci whose figures were more subtle, and gentler perhaps, than the work of Kandler at Meissen. Teawares were painted with spirited

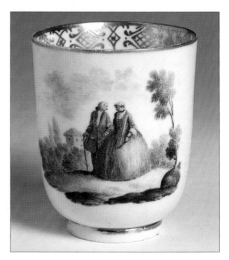

Capodimonte's combination of creaminess with subtlety gives this cup by Guiseppe della Torre a very special feel. c.1750.

Early Naples figures follow the tradition of Capodimonte with a special charm as well as careful attention to detail. 7½in. (19cm), crowned N mark, c.1790.

battle scenes, figures in pretty landscapes, and scenes from the Italian Comedy, painted with delicate stippling by painters trained as miniaturists. Minutely painted snuff boxes and tiny cups are a joy to hold, for the glaze has a softness and delicacy rivalled only by Vincennes and the earliest Chelsea.

The mark used at Capodimonte was the fleur-de-lis, usually in blue, taken from the Bourbon arms. It is worth remembering that the emblem of the crowned N of Naples was never used at Capodimonte. Victorian collectors confused later eighteenth century products of the Royal Naples factory with the legendary earlier porcelain, This gave rise to a confusion that exists to the present, whereby nineteenth century copies of Doccia are today known as Capodimonte (see the previous entry). The many modern Italian factories making bisque figural ornaments have absolutely no connection with the original Capodimonte.

Further reading

Alice Frothingham Thomas: *Capo di Monte and Buen Retiro Porcelains,* New York, 1955

4. NAPLES

Often referred to as Fabbrica Reale Ferdinandea,

the Royal Factory at Naples was established by Ferdinand IV in 1771 and survived until 1806. Ferdinand hoped to recreate the fine porcelain made by his father, Charles III; indeed, in Naples a soft paste porcelain was made by some of the craftsmen who had worked previously at Capodimonte and so there is a distinct resemblance.

Fashions had changed, however, and Naples porcelain was dominated by the new classical taste. Excavations at nearby Pompeii and Herculaneum influenced both the shape and decoration of Naples porcelain which was always made to the highest standards. Topographical painting of local views and finely painted portraits were specialities, as well as biscuit portrait busts and medallions. Naples porcelain was marked with the emblem of the King, either FRF or the letter N below a crown, painted in underglaze blue and usually smudged below the creamy bubbled glaze. Later in the nineteenth century the crowned N mark was used on copies of Doccia and other Italian porcelain which was sold using the name of Capodimonte. Genuine Naples porcelain is rare and costly.

Further reading

Francesco Stazzi: *Italian Porcelain,* 1967

CHAPTER 9

FRANCE

The early porcelain of France is refreshingly different from Oriental imports, for the designs are European, copying silver shapes and patterns of baroque *lambrequins* borrowed from architecture, metalwork and faïence. Kaolin had not been discovered and so French chemists developed their own kind of *pâte tendre* or soft paste porcelain, creamy and smooth with the delicacy of ivory-tinted glass.

The early history of French porcelain is not fully understood, but manufacture was perfected at Rouen at least as early as the 1680s, using a patent granted to Louis Proterat in 1673. Proterat took his secrets with him when he died in 1696 and only a small number of pieces with formal blue decoration can be ascribed to Rouen. These greatly influenced the early products of the first successful European porcelain factory, established at St Cloud by the Chicaneau family who produced a warm, creamy soft paste by 1695. Direct copies of Dehua *blanc de chine* were made

French soft paste porcelain, or pâte tendre, represented by a Chantilly inkstand, c.1740, a Vincennes sucrier dated 1753, and a Mennecy pot-pourri vase c.1760. All are typically French.

A pair of Sèvres plates from the service ordered by Louis Philippe for his sister to use at the Château de Randon. The flower painting is by Jacques Sinsson, 9½in. (24cm), dated 1839.

alongside blue and white, especially beakers with secure *trembleuse* saucers, and large quantities of cutlery handles, some enamelled with Chinese figures.

Very similar designs were made at Chantilly, where a porcelain factory was founded by the Prince de Condé in 1725. The principal influences at Chantilly were *chinoiserie* and Japanese Kakiemon, for the decorators copied Oriental porcelain from the Prince's private collection. The early glaze used at Chantilly is opaque due to the addition of tin oxide, a unique material of unrivalled beauty.

Another nobleman, the Duc de Villeroy, established a porcelain factory in Paris which transferred to Mennecy in 1748. Mennecy porcelain was particularly creamy and soft, ideally suited to the French rococo decoration that was painted in a delicate palette.

The King of France, Louis XV, desired to make his own porcelain and personally financed a factory at the Royal Château at Vincennes. To protect his investment the King issued a Royal Edict severely restricting the activities of all other porcelain factories in France, forbidding existing makers from using gold and certain colours in their decoration, and preventing all workmen at Vincennes from joining any rival china works. With immense subsidy from the Royal Court, Vincennes porcelain was a guaranteed success, and the quality of its products was protected by the most careful inspection. Anything other than the most perfect porcelain was discarded and stored in vast warehouses until after the Revolution. The Vincennes works were transferred to Sèvres in 1756 but production continued without change. The factory specialised in smooth, solid ground colours enriched with tooled gilding which framed panels painted with scenes and flowers, the colours sinking into the soft white glaze. Shapes and patterns were totally original, epitomising the French rococo, and of course Sèvres porcelain exerted a great influence on all other European porcelain.

Pâte tendre continued to be made until the end of the eighteenth century, although hard paste, the so-called *pâte duré*, was made alongside soft paste at Sèvres from 1769.

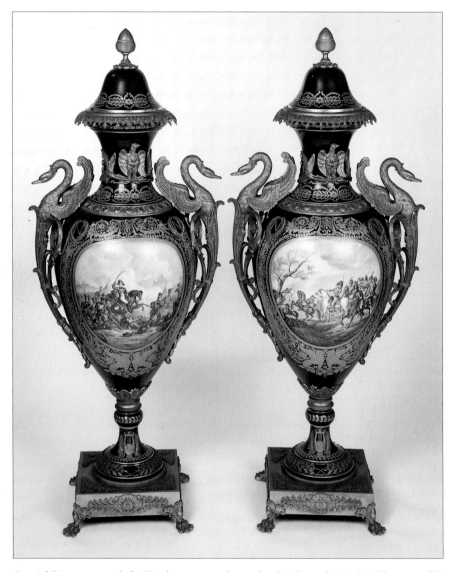

Imperial Sèvres vases made for Napoleon were much reproduced in France late in the 19th century. This magnificent pair, 44in. (112cm) high, is probably by Samson of Paris.

French hard paste porcelain is beautifully white, and its perfection led to a most important industry based around Paris and Limoges. The relaxation of the royal edict in 1766 enabled other factories to develop porcelain that rivalled the quality of Sèvres, and fierce competition developed in Paris in particular. With the backing of successive Republican and Royal governments, Sèvres continued to make the highest quality porcelain throughout the nineteenth century and up to the present day. Other factories produced wares aimed at cheaper markets, while at the same time a great number of china painters working in Paris decorated porcelain in the richest and most opulent taste, ornamented with the most brilliant gold borders and backgrounds.

French fashion dictated the taste of most of Europe. Paris porcelain had a profound influence on the porcelain made in England, Germany and Bohemia, and even Russia and the United States. The *Empire* style was universal across different continents and without makers' marks nineteenth century porcelain is almost impossible to attribute. A great deal of French porcelain is unmarked, and this discourages collectors. As a result, many very decorative French porcelain items can be realistically priced, especially pieces in the revived rococo style of the 1830s and 1840s.

Most of the porcelain decorated in Paris was made at Limoges where a fine white clay and kaolin deposits were discovered in the eighteenth century. After the decline of Paris as the porcelain capital of France, Limoges grew to rival Stoke-on-Trent as a major porcelain producer. An enormous market was discovered in the United States and Canada where inexpensive Limoges was used in every household including The White House. Much of the later Limoges porcelain was derivative, and a great use has been made of very cheap photo-litho printing for souvenir items. In addition, however, some exciting original Art Deco designs were made in the 1920s. Much of the later French porcelain copies old Paris and Sèvres patterns, frequently with fake factory marks. Some Sèvres style pieces can still be very decorative and expensive, especially Bettignie porcelain made at Tournai and enamelled in Paris. The Samson factory is maligned for making endless fakes of early porcelain, but in terms of the quality of its productions, Samson deserves to stand on its own.

A St Cloud spice box with a revolving lid, painted in typically bright blue, 5½in. (14cm) wide, c.1730.

1. ST CLOUD

St Cloud, a small concern run by Pierre Chicaneau and his family, is important as the first commercially viable European porcelain.

The date of the earliest production is uncertain, but it was probably perfected by 1695, influenced by experiments at Rouen. The creamy frit porcelain was hard to control in the kiln and so the factory avoided plates and anything large. One of the joys of St Cloud is its small scale, for it specialised in snuffboxes, cane handles and cutlery handles. Beakers and teabowls often sit on *trembleuse* saucers with a moulded ridge to hold the cup securely without tipping over. These shapes are not Chinese and the blue and white decoration is also very French, influenced by the *lambrequin* scroll patterns associated with the designer Bérain. Coloured wares copied Japanese Kakiemon and also *chinoiserie* figures – fanciful and fun. Some pieces are marked with the initials St C over T incised or in blue, occasionally with a sun face, marks copied later by Samson in hard paste, stained to look creamy and soft.

Porcelain was made at St Cloud until the 1760s, but later productions are hard to identify and generally of little merit.

Further reading
W.B. Honey: *French Porcelain,* 1950
George Savage: *Seventeenth & Eighteenth Century French Porcelain,* 1960

A Chantilly double-handled sauceboat in the delightful creamy soft paste porcelain. The decoration in Kakiemon style, c.1735-40.

2. CHANTILLY

The Prince de Condé, Louis-Henri de Bourbon, was one of a special breed of European noblemen who established porcelain factories as an extension of their hobby of collecting Japanese and Chinese ceramics.

Production began at Chantilly in about 1725, but without access to kaolin necessary to make true porcelain to rival the Prince's beloved Kakiemon. Instead, the creamy frit porcelain of Chantilly was coated with a tin oxide-based glaze that whitened it and gave it a unique feel, somewhere between porcelain and faïence. Once you have handled early Chantilly porcelain, the appearance is unmistakable. So too is the decoration. Old Japanese Kakiemon in the Prince's collection inspired the colouring, while patterns were often copied from Chinese blue and white, the images transformed into rich Japan style enamels.

A neatly painted hunting horn in red is a mark to be treated with respect, for the quality and taste of 1730s Chantilly is exemplary. Competition from the King's factory at Vincennes and the enforced Royal Edict of 1745 brought to an abrupt end all that was fine. Porcelain continued to be made at Chantilly until the very end of the eighteenth century, especially blue and white plates with simple sprig patterns which sold well, but these are a poor reminder of former glory. Samson copies of Chantilly, complete with red hunting horn marks, greatly outnumber genuine pieces, so collectors need to be careful.

Further reading

Geoffrey Godden: *Guide to European Porcelain,* 1993

George Savage: *Seventeenth & Eighteenth Century French Porcelain,* 1960

3. MENNECY AND BOURG-LA-REINE

After a promising start in 1734 in the Rue de Charonne in Paris, the factory which transferred to Mennecy in 1748 fell victim to the Royal Edict designed to protect the King's factory at Vincennes. Forbidden from using gold and with a restricted market, Mennecy can feel like an inferior French porcelain but it is not without its charm. The factory

A 'Pagod' figure made at Mennecy to replace popular figures previously brought from China. The decoration is fanciful chinoiserie, 4¼in. (11cm), marked DV.

specialised in custard cups and miniature vases that possibly served a similar purpose. Also a great variety of porcelain snuffboxes were made. The colouring is as soft as the glaze, a rose pink enamel usually prominent in any decoration. The rims are often edged in this same muddy pink instead of gold. A range of charming figures was made but these were often crudely painted and are far more successful when left in the white.

The factory was owned by the Duc de Villeroy, Louis-François de Neufville, and his initials, DV, were used as a mark at Paris, Mennecy and also at Bourg-la-Reine where the works moved for a final time in 1773. The Mennecy name is generally used for porcelain from all periods of the Duc's factory, however. The same creamy paste and range of colours

were continued at Bourg-la-Reine, but the quality declined noticeably. Porcelain was abandoned and earthenware only was made until about 1806.

Further reading
W.B. Honey: *French Porcelain,* 1950
George Savage: *Seventeenth & Eighteenth Century French Porcelain,* 1960

4. VINCENNES AND SEVRES

Experimental production began at the Château of Vincennes about 1738 with backing from the King. Gentle progress had been made by 1745 when the King prohibited by law all foreign porcelain imports into France except for Chinese goods. Furthermore, all other French china makers were now forbidden from using certain enamel colours and any gilding on their porcelain. This enforced monopoly was very unfair on Chantilly, Mennecy and other established factories, but it guaranteed the success of the King's venture and led to some of the world's most beautiful porcelain

A Sèvres sucrier painted by the distinctive hand of the artist André-Vincent Vielliard, the marks identifying the painter and the date of manufacture, letter O for 1767, 4in. (10cm) high. Sandon collection

which may never have been possible without the prestigious backing of the French Court. Free of commercial pressures, the factory could concentrate on quality above all else, porcelain truly to rival the Royal Saxon China from Meissen.

The porcelain of Vincennes and Sèvres – where the growing factory was moved to in 1753 – captures perfectly the mood of French rococo. Gentle, feminine shapes, bold colours that are pleasing, not shocking, and careful paintings that blend on to the silky glaze with a special delicacy. The gilding lies thick and warm upon the surface and individual tooling adds to the richness like jewelled frames around a picture. Sèvres is famed for its coloured grounds, much imitated but never bettered. *Gros bleu* is an intense underglaze blue that was hard to control, but quite dramatic. *Bleu celeste* is a sparkling turquoise that forms wonderful borders. A deep rose pink, an apple green and a brilliant yellow are scarce and valuable colours when authentic, but fakes abound.

To collect Sèvres it is necessary first of all to study the subject in detail in order to avoid numerous traps for the unwary. We are helped by the most detailed marking system of any porcelain factory. The year of making and the name of the potter, painter and gilder of every piece was recorded in a special code alongside the factory mark – the Royal cipher of King Louis XV.

Fine eighteenth century Sèvres is naturally expensive, but there are still plenty of examples available at less than £200, painted with coloured flowers on the delicate white ground. Vast services were made with simple flower patterns, many pieces of which were subjected to later redecoration involving the fraudulent addition of far more valuable ground colours. It is, therefore, most important that novice collectors buy only from specialist dealers and leading auction rooms. At the other extreme, though, it is by no means unusual for perfectly genuine early pieces to be mistakenly sold as late copies for a fraction of their true worth. Once kaolin had been discovered in France, Sèvres made a truc hard paste porcelain from 1768. By this time, however, the soft paste had already become legendary and customers preferred it. Consequently both bodies were made alongside one another up until the nineteenth century when the soft paste was finally abandoned.

Although the French Revolution deposed many of the factory's aristocratic customers, the new governments still looked upon the state porcelain factory as a valued asset. Fine services were made for Napoleon, including the celebrated Egyptian service subsequently presented to the Duke of Wellington.

The factory survived into the twentieth century and continues today, although later production was never massive, concentrating on quality rather than quantity. Notable products reflect the French spirits of Art Nouveau and Art Deco, decorative vases and dramatic figures that are rarely given the appreciation they deserve. Instead, nineteenth century Sèvres is destined to be forever confused with the abundance of fakes made in Limoges and Paris in the style of the previous greatness. Mostly made in hard paste, the copies by Samson and other French factories can be highly decorative and are often expensive. Owners of such pieces are greatly concerned to find their costly purchases

An early Sèvres small tray combining the distinctive Rose Pompadour *and* Pomme Verte *ground colours, 4¼in. (11cm), dated 1760.*

Sèvres continued into the 20th century and maintained high quality under pressure. This 1940s service was made for Reichsmarschall Goering's fiftieth birthday.

condemned by experts as forgeries. It is probably right to think of these not as fakes but as reproductions, and the fine products made in soft paste porcelain by the Bettignies family regularly command four figure sums on their quality alone.

Further reading

Sir Geoffrey de Bellaigue and S. Eriksen: *Sèvres Porcelain*

John Sandon: *The Story of Porcelain,* 1996

Rosalind Savill: *The Wallace Collection, Catalogue of Sèvres Porcelain,* 3 volumes, 1988

5. PARIS PORCELAIN

Veaux Paris or 'Old Paris' is a generic term to describe the products of numerous factories and decorating establishments in and around Paris between about 1780 and 1840. Because of intense competition, the bigger makers proudly marked their names on their pieces, but a great deal was left unmarked. The situation is further complicated because decorators bought glazed white porcelain 'blanks from the same factories in Limoges, and so identical shapes can occur with different name marks. The enforced monopoly Sèvres had enjoyed for fine work

The brilliance of Paris gilding was rarely equalled. These centrepieces of Limoges biscuit porcelain were decorated in Neppel's Parisian workshop, c.1810-15.

using rich gilding finally came to an end at the French Revolution. Just prior to this other factories had been permitted to make hard paste porcelain sets with simple border patterns and sprig designs, very popular in France in the 1780s and '90s and exported in quantity to London and elsewhere.

After the turmoil of revolution, Paris blossomed around 1800 as a centre of excellence. Lavish table sets were made in the richest taste, influenced by the contemporary products of Sèvres. It is difficult to generalise, for Paris porcelain was made to suit every level of the market, but the quality of the pure white porcelain is consistently high, with bright gold shining from every border and rim. Deep blue was also widely used as a background. The principal taste was known as *Empire*, mixing influences of ancient Greece, Rome and Egypt with bright colours and gilding. In addition to table services, teasets and *déjeuner* sets on trays, Paris is famed for pairs of vases, the handles in the form of winged caryatids or

dolphins, or cabinet cups and saucers with similarly lavish handles and superb painted panels emblazoned on the front.

The factories were known either by the name of their proprietor (or chief patron), or else by the street in Paris where they had their shop. The makers are too numerous to list here, but names to watch out for as the most important in terms of quality productions include the factories of The Duc d'Angoulême (run by Dihl & Guerhard); Dagoty (also Dagoty & Honoré); Darte Frères; Feuillet; Halley; Locre (known as La Courtille); Monsieur (known as Clignancourt); Nast; Neppel; Potter (known as Rue de Crussol); The Queen's Factory (in Rue Thiroux under the patronage of Marie Antoinette); Schoelcher; and Stone, Coquerel & Legros.

Because of the hard glaze, the gold on Paris porcelain is prone to wear, and collectors should watch out for pieces which have been re-gilded as there is no substitute for the brilliance of original Paris gilding.

Further reading

Geoffrey Godden: *Guide to European Porcelain,* 1993

Regine de Plinval de Guillebon: *Paris Porcelain 1770-1850,* 1972

6. JACOB PETIT

The factory of Jacob Petit is one of the most important and best known in France. The works had been established in Paris around 1830 and from humble beginnings became a major producer of ornamental ware in the new revived rococo taste which replaced *Empire* during the 1830s. Petit understood the new fashion perfectly and due to increased production, the works were transferred to larger premises in Fontainebleau in about 1834.

Clock cases and cornucopia vases awash with heavily moulded leaf scrolls and applied china flowers typify the Fontainebleau porcelain which was not as delicate as Dresden or Coalbrookdale of similar date. Nevertheless, Jacob Petit's porcelain found great favour in England as well as France for it was highly decorative, the somewhat eccentric modelling picked out in bright colours and gold. Perfume bottles in the shape of china figurines, and novelty *veilleuses* or coffee warmers, were specialities of the factory and can show much ingenuity in design. Jacob Petit has been often accused of bad taste, but it was the popular taste of the time and was well made and designed to last. One advantage of the heavily moulded style is that damage is easily lost among the wealth of decoration and so detracts less than on simpler porcelain. Pieces were normally marked clearly with the letters J.P. in underglaze blue, although copies of Meissen marks were also used, leading to confusion with the products of Dresden. Jacob Petit sold his works in 1862 and died four years later.

Further reading

Antoinette Fay-Halle and Barbara Mundt: *Nineteenth Century European Porcelain,* 1983
Geoffrey Godden: *Guide to European Porcelain,* 1993

The rococo style was well suited to Jacob Petit's coloured grounds with raised gilding. This cut flower vase dates from the 1840s, 8in. (20.5cm).

7. PORCELAINE DE PARIS

I refer here to a single porcelain factory in Paris, originating in the eighteenth century and run by the Clauss family from 1822 and the Bloch family from 1887, continuing to the present day as Porcelaine de Paris SA. The name is hardly known, but its products are abundant, masquerading as Meissen or Dresden, or confused with the output of the Samson factory.

Porcelaine de Paris specialised in copies of established porcelain makers, especially Meissen, Sèvres or Capodimonte, and used imitation marks rather than their own name. I am frequently shown large figures and candelabra, believed by their owners to be genuine products of the Meissen factory, and I have to break the news that these are Clauss copies, made by this enterprising French

Porcelaine de Paris in the Dresden taste, bearing a copy of the Meissen mark. A fake, maybe, but reasonably well made and decorative, even in white. 18¾in. (48cm).

factory which played to the gullibility of English customers. Prevented from copying the contemporary mark still in use at Meissen, the Clausses marked their figures with the crossed swords with either a dot or star, as used during the Academic or Marcolini periods half a century before.

The porcelain is very white and can be distinguished from Meissen by the omission of

incised marks and the use of pads and fine clay grit to support the bases of figures during the firing. Porcelaine de Paris figures were often sold in the white, shining with a brilliant glaze. At their best they are highly decorative, but the factory is destined to remain in obscurity due to its choice to forge other markers' marks rather than develop a style of its own.

Further reading
Michel Bloit: *Trois Siècles de Porcelaine de Paris,* 1988

8. GILLE AND VION & BAURY

Jean Marie Gille established a porcelain factory in Paris in the 1830s, specialising in bisque porcelain figures in the Dresden style. During the 1850s and '60s the factory grew to a considerable size and exhibited at every major international exhibition, receiving widespread acclaim for the quality of its productions. While the modelling can appear clumsy, Gille figures are notable for the care with which they were enamelled, the costumes painted with delicate patterns in bright colours and tooled gold. The factory traded as Gille Jeune and used the mark of an embossed blue clay pad bearing a cipher which can be read as either GJ or JG.

One of Gille's principal modellers, Charles Baury, took over the factory on Gille's death in 1868 and continued the works with August Vion as Vion and Baury, having moved to Choisy le Roi. Fine coloured bisque figures continued to be made, marked now with the raised letters VB. In addition some figures were sold in white unglazed bisque and others in glazed white porcelain, marked with a large anchor in green. The works closed in about 1880. Jean Gille and Vion & Baury figures have never regained the popularity they enjoyed during the last century and, considering their exceptional decoration, deserve to be far more expensive than they are today.

Further reading
Geoffrey Godden: *Guide to European Porcelain,* 1993

French biscuit figures by Gille, typical of this factory's high quality productions, 15¼in. (39cm), c.1860.

9. LIMOGES

Frequently referred to as the 'Stoke-on-Trent of France', Limoges became the centre of the French porcelain industry owing to the deposits of kaolin found nearby. Numerous porcelain makers established themselves here, beginning with the Comte d'Artois' factory in the 1780s. Large amounts of white Limoges porcelain were sent to Paris for decorating, and

it was not until the late nineteenth century that any sizeable output of porcelain was marketed as having come from Limoges.

The success of Limoges relied on its exploitation of the American market, led by an American dealer, David Haviland. Haviland began making his own porcelain in Limoges from about 1853, and the firm has continued to be run by his family as Haviland & Co. up until modern times. The history is confused by

A dish from a Limoges dessert service, c.1910, with careful use of litho printing, 11¾in. (30cm).

different family members trading at times on their own, as C.F. Haviland and Theodore Haviland, all making very similar productions. Other principal porcelain makers in Limoges include the firms of Julien Balleroy & Cie, G.D.A., J. Granger & Cie and M. Redon of La Porcelaine Limousine.

Later Limoges porcelain is always clearly marked with the full name or initials of the maker. Limoges is best known for tea and dessert services which were enormously popular in Britain and America in the 1890s and early 1900s. Delicate grounds shaded by aerographing were heightened with the use of raised paste gilding in the style of Royal Worcester or Vienna, and printed flowers were lightly coloured-in on similar shaded grounds. Some of the best raised gilding is worthy of close examination, but most Limoges services

were aimed at mass markets and were simply good, everyday decoration. A lot of white Limoges porcelain was sent to America and Australia for the use of independent china painters, ranging from amateurs to very competent workshops.

In more recent times Limoges has become famous for miniature porcelain novelties, decorated with copies of famous paintings, but, despite the presence of 'signatures', these are printed photographically and are merely inexpensive toys. Limoges porcelain is widely collected in the United States but generally undervalued in Britain.

Further reading

Mary Frank Gaston: *The Collectors Encyclopaedia of Limoges Porcelain,* 1980, revised 1992

The quality of decoration on this late Tournai cup and saucer is the equal of Sèvres from fifty years before, but with fake marks it remains just a glorious reproduction, decorated in Paris in the mid-19th century.

10. TOURNAI AND ST AMAND LES EAUX

Tournai porcelain is essentially French, although the factory was established in Flanders by François-Joseph Peterinck in 1751. The creamy soft paste closely resembles Sèvres, and the decoration of delicate flowers or puce landscapes also has a distinct Sèvres feel to it. Biscuit and glazed figures were made with careful attention to detail, and there are many links with English porcelain as some of the painters and modellers engaged at Tournai also worked at Chelsea and Derby. Tournai's best known service, painted with birds on a rich blue ground for the Duc d'Orléans in 1787, is as fine as any from Sèvres. Late eighteenth century Tournai is, however, dominated by cheap blue and white dinner services with simple sprig patterns. The factory

mark was either a simple tower or crossed swords with four small crosses, in blue or gold.

In the nineteenth century there was a great demand for Sèvres porcelain and a ready market for fakes. The old Tournai factory was reopened in the 1840s by a former worker, Maximilien Bettignies, who subsequently moved the works to the French town of St Amand les Eaux. Between 1850 and 1870 copies were made of eighteenth century Sèvres cabinet wares, ornamented with raised enamel jewelling by independent decorators in Paris. Some were undoubtedly passed off as genuine Sèvres, but most of the copies sold simply because they were pretty and of high quality.

Lady Charlotte Schreiber visited Tournai and St Amand les Eaux in 1877 and described the production of fakes, especially copies of Chelsea and Worcester, with deep blue or scale blue grounds and wonderful gilding. Because

A Tournai figure of a young cobbler, 6¼in. (16cm), c.1760. The delightful, soft creamy feel of French soft paste is seen at its most gentle on white porcelain figures.

they are soft paste these copies of English porcelain are much more convincing than Samson's copies. It was claimed Bettignies' porcelain was not intended to deceive, for the decorators added their own initials to the Sèvres marks in place of date letters – C for the decorator Caille, L for Lehujeur and BB for Bareau and Bareau. More than a century later many of Bettignies' pieces are treasured as priceless old Sèvres, but they are very well made and should not be condemned as mere fakes. Pretty jewelled cups and saucers regularly sell for well over £1,000 each, the price of serious porcelain.

Further reading

W.B. Honey: *French Porcelain,* 1950
Geoffrey Godden: *Guide to European Porcelain,* 1993

11. SAMSON

Samson is probably the most famous French porcelain factory after Sèvres itself, and certainly one of the most prolific. Its products still fool experts and amateurs alike, for Samson copies are technically superior to most of the originals they set out to imitate.

The firm was established in 1845 by Edmé Samson and continued by his son Emile. They began as decorators in the Rue Béranger in Paris and it is not certain when Samson first made its own porcelain. The works reproduced every kind of collectable porcelain from the past, and there is hardly a single type of Continental, English or Oriental china that was not exactly copied.

The skill of this notorious faker has to be admired, for many pieces capture perfectly the spirit of the originals and match exactly the appearance of the glaze and colours. Samson used a typical Paris hard paste porcelain; consequently, in order to copy English or French soft pastes, chemicals were added to the glaze to give it a false creaminess. Some nineteenth century Samson used a glaze containing uranium which today fluoresces a brilliant yellow under ultraviolet light. This can come as a shock to many owners of porcelain believed to be old Meissen or Chantilly, but such a test is not foolproof as only a small part of the factory's output used this fluorescent glaze. Mostly it takes experience to tell when you are looking at a piece of Samson.

It was claimed that Samson marked every piece with its own sign – a cursive cross made up of the letter S mirrored. This mark is often encountered, but the majority of Samson is unmarked apart from a copy of the mark found on the original.

In addition to porcelain, Samson also made high quality ormolu and copied enamels, delft and faïence. I have heard that Samson is sought after in its own right, but I know of very few collectors. Some pieces do command high prices, not because of who made them, but because of their sheer quality and decorative merit (see page 70). Instead of receiving the praise it deserves, Samson's name is debased in many people's minds by the endless range of

The tailor's wife on a goat, complete with a carefully painted Derby mark of 1810-20 and authentic decoration, but the hard paste porcelain body identifies this as a Samson forgery, made c.1900, 6¾in. (17.5cm).

cheap Continental reproductions generically known as 'Samson'. It is really ironic that such a well-known forger should today have inferior products passed off as its own.

Good Samson figures are well worth collecting as they are reasonably priced for the work in them. It is also not difficult to learn how to tell 'real' Samson.

The firm stopped making porcelain in the 1970s and the vast works collection, some 4,000 pieces, was sold by auction in a series of now famous sales at Christie's in London.

Further reading

Geoffrey Godden: *Guide to European Porcelain*, 1993

CHAPTER 10

GERMANY

INTRODUCTION

The dream of European porcelain was realised in Baroque Germany by an alchemist, Johann Friedrich Böttger. Having failed the King of Prussia because he could not manufacture gold, Böttger fled to Saxony and was promptly imprisoned by Augustus the Strong. Realising gold was beyond even Böttger's capability, Augustus set him the task of emulating the white porcelain of China. Assisting the chemist Ehrenfried von Tschirnhausen, Bottger built primitive kilns at Dresden where initially a hard red stoneware

was produced, known as *Böttger Steinzeug*. The first true porcelain to be made in Europe was perfected by 1710. Backing from porcelain-mad Augustus ensured the success of the venture and a new factory was built at Meissen, twelve miles from Dresden.

Uneven firing and the creamy appearance of the early Böttger porcelain was gradually eradicated and by the 1720s 'Dresden China' made at Meissen was treasured throughout Europe. The glaze was smoother and whiter than most Chinese porcelain and rivalled the celebrated Kakiemon from Japan. Augustus saw little need to copy the Chinese directly and

A Meissen group of the Spanish Lovers, 8½in. (21.5cm), c.1745-50. J.J. Kändler captured movement and imagination, while dramatic colouring and an original French ormolu rococo base work together to perfection.

Der Sommer. A Berlin plaque by L Knoeller framed with its own Vienna style border. 14in. x 20in. (36cm. x 51cm), KPM mark, c.1890. This copy of a well-known painting by Makaert is more decorative than any oil painting.

instead his factory developed new decorative styles partly inspired by the Orient but totally different. The principal theme was *Chinoiserie,* led by the painters Stadler, von Lowenfinck and especially Johann Gregor Herold. European flowers *(deutsche Blumen)* and landscapes appealed to different tastes and armorials were carefully added for special customers. Modelling was of great importance during the 1730s and '40s and Meissen's success was due to the genius of Johann Joachim Kändler, the inventor of the china figurine as we know it today. No other sculptor's work has been so influential and so widely copied throughout the world.

Other kings and noblemen, jealous of Augustus' success, wanted porcelain factories of their own. In spite of lengthy precautions, disgruntled and greedy employees were enticed away from Meissen, bringing with them knowledge of Böttger's secrets. Claudius

du Paquier established a porcelain factory in Vienna by 1718 using the recipe brought from Meissen by Samuel Stolzel. Stolzel's assistant, Christoph Hunger, joined Vezzi in Venice soon afterwards and inevitably there is a similarity between these early porcelains. Subsequently Joseph Ringler was paramount in spreading the art of porcelain making across Germany. Ringler had discovered the secret while working as a painter at Vienna, and he provided the technical knowledge needed to establish factories at Höchst, Frankenthal, Nymphenburg and Ludwigsburg. Ringer's assistant from Höchst, Johann Benckgraff, was enticed away by the King of Prussia to join his factory in Berlin in 1752, before leaving for Furstenberg and the Duke of Brunswick three years later. Apart from Ludwigsburg (which had a tendency to fire somewhat smoky or brown), all of the major German factories made a similar 'True' or 'Hard Paste' porcelain

A richly decorated Dresden plate from the Lamm workshop, made for the American market, 10¾in. (27.5cm), c.1910.

A German lace dancer, 6¾in. (17cm), c.1920-30. Decorated with real lacework, dipped in porcelain clay and applied before firing, this was an inexpensive and popular ornament.

just as white as Meissen, decorated in what became a generic German taste. If it was not for the widespread use of factory marks, telling one German maker from another would be a tricky task indeed.

Early German porcelain makers mastered Baroque and Rococo. After a less dramatic Classical phase, the spirit of Rococo in its most flamboyant form dominated German porcelain again in the nineteenth century. Meissen found that original figure subjects by Kändler continued to sell in great numbers, especially in England where many can be found today. English customers loved German porcelain, but were confused about where precisely it came from. Meissen was known as Dresden and subsequently many other makers in the Dresden area used the same term for their copies of traditional Meissen designs. Independent decorators, headed by Helena Wolfsohn, capitalised on the confusion by using copies of old Meissen

marks. Consequently the name Dresden has come to represent a style only, typified today by table centrepieces supported by china Cupids and encrusted with dainty modelled roses. The same is true of Vienna, as, following the closure of the State factory in 1864, anyone was free to use the well-known shield mark on porcelain in Vienna style. Quality of workmanship is far more important than who actually made a piece of 'Vienna' or 'Dresden'.

From the late nineteenth century, German industrial mass-production led to a vast output of inexpensive, decorative porcelain. Novelty 'fairings' and pairs of cheap bisque figurines adorned the mantelpieces of homes all over the world, while 'ribbon plates' with colour-printed pictures were hung from their pierced rims on everyone's wall. In no way can such pieces be considered works of art, but most have brought enormous pleasure to many generations of owners.

Schwarzlot *decoration (painted in black monochrome) emphasises the pure whiteness of early Meissen porcelain. This example was painted in Ignatz Preissler's independent china-painting workshop in Breslau, and is known as* Hausmalerei; *6¼in. (16cm) high, c.1730.*

1. MEISSEN

The first European 'True' or Hard Paste porcelain was the personal obsession of Augustus the Strong, King of Saxony, a porcelain collector who more than anything wanted a china factory of his own. Augustus was losing patience with his chief chemist, Ehrenfried von Tschirnhausen who had struggled in vain to manufacture porcelain. The breakthrough came with the arrival of Johann Friedrich Böttger, a young alchemist fleeing from neighbouring Prussia. Virtually imprisoned in Augustus' castle, Böttger and von Tschirnhausen initially produced a high-fired red stoneware, as fine as the Yixing ware from China. This hard red body could be polished on a lapidary wheel to give it a unique feel, and vessels were mounted in gold or set with precious gems. Although not porcelain,

Böttger Stoneware today constitutes the most valuable of all early Meissen productions. Von Tschirnhausen died in 1708, just as his gifted assistant made his first experimental porcelain, using a white china clay (kaolin) from Kolditz. To develop this, Böttger encouraged Augustus to erect a new factory at Meissen, producing white 'Böttger Porcelain' from 1710.

A new source of kaolin discovered at Aue rectified some early problems and gradually the creamy appearance of Böttger Porcelain was replaced by a pure white body and glaze as smooth as the Japanese Kakiemon much loved by Augustus. Early Meissen copied the Orient, although blue and white proved difficult. The best porcelain was sold just in white with embossed decoration of acanthus leaves or modelled flowers. This was sent to Augsburg for mounting in silver and gold and many pieces were enamelled by independent painters

The Chinese lovers, modelled by Peter Reinicke and made at Meissen, c.1745. This is the epitome of German chinoiserie. 4⅜in. (11cm) high, crossed swords mark.

or Hausmalers in Augsburg and Breslau. The most famous independent decorating workshops, those of the Seuter and Auffenwerth families, were responsible for *chinoiserie* and European painting far superior to anything enamelled at Meissen. Internal disagreement held up progress, and Böttger's assistant Samuel Stolzel defected to the rival factory at Vienna. Following Böttger's death in 1719, a commission was appointed to continue the Meissen factory and Stolzel was enticed back with the offer of more money. He brought with him from Vienna Johann Gregor Herold, a talented painter who was also a gifted chemist.

Herold was placed in charge of decoration at Meissen and developed a new palette of bright enamel colours. Herold painted some pieces himself with fanciful *chinoiserie,* and he also produced drawings to be copied by others. Consequently it is difficult to distinguish the hand of J.G. Herold from that of his pupils, especially his kinsman Christian Friedrich Herold. Other senior painters also had pupils working in their style. Adam Friedrich von Lowenfinck painted fanciful beasts called *Fabeltiere,* while Johann Ehrenfried Stadler painted cartoon chinamen in a very different manner from Herold. Johann Gottfried Klinger painted flowers and insects *ombrierte* where the painting appears to cast shadows on to the porcelain. His careful painting of real flowers developed into Meissen's most popular decoration, the so-called *deutsche Blumen* or German Flowers. Meanwhile *indianische Blumen* or 'Indian' style flowers were derived from China and Japan. European landscape artists included C.F. Herold, Johann Georg Heintze and Bonaventura Gottlieb Häuer who is best known for his paintings of miners. The work of these Meissen painters was copied in due course by most other European porcelain factories.

Figures were among the earliest productions at Meissen. From 1727 a series of fantastic white porcelain animals were made for Augustus' new 'Japanese' palace, initially the work of Johann Gottlob Kirchner and completed by Johann Joachim Kändler. Kändler became the most important single artist involved with the Meissen factory, for his modelling brought figure making into a totally new dimension. He could turn his hand to any subject the public desired, Saints and street vendors, harlequins and harlots, Immortals and inebriates, all perfectly to scale and full of movement and character. Kandler had many pupils and a great many followers, as all other German factories copied Meissen figures and the distinctive manner in which they were coloured. The enamels were bright, but plenty of white porcelain was always left showing, for this was Meissen's pride.

On the death of Augustus in 1733, another larger-than-life character was put in charge of the Meissen factory. Count Heinrich von Bruhl is best remembered for the 'Swan Service', an incredible table decoration created for him by Kändler in 1738, and for the model of his tailor seated on a goat, also designed to sit on Count Bruhl's table as a joke. During the 1740s Meissen still lacked serious competition and expanded into new markets especially in Turkey and Russia. All was to change during the Seven Years War (1756-63) when Saxony was overrun by Prussia and Meissen fell into the hands of Frederick the Great. Frederick took many of the best workmen to his own porcelain factory in Berlin, but Kändler

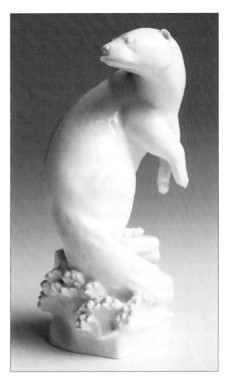

A Meissen model of an otter by Max Esser, 10in. (25cm), c.1930. The sculptural quality of Meissen's white porcelain was re-discovered in the 20th century.   Sandon collection

remained at Meissen and extensive orders were placed by Frederick himself to prevent the factory's decline. After the war in 1763 the so-called 'Academic' period of the factory commenced with the appointment of a painter, Christian Dietrich, as Art Director. Kändler finally retired and new modellers updated Meissen's productions in the face of competition from other German factories.

The famous mark of the crossed swords of Saxony was used from 1722. Early marks were often in blue enamel overglaze, but from the late 1720s most pieces were marked with the sign in blue underglaze. Special pieces bore other signs connected with the King, the letters KPM or the personal AR cipher for Augustus

Rex. These marks were much imitated in the nineteenth century. The precise shape of the crossed swords mark gives a vital clue to the date of manufacture. The early swords are thin and straight and crossed almost at right angles, whereas in the nineteenth century they tend to curve and cross at an acute angle. Dark pommels on the sword hilts normally indicate a nineteenth century date. During the academic period (1763-1774) a dot was placed between the sword hilts and consequently this period is also known as the 'Dot Period'. In 1774 Count Camillo Marcolini became director at Meissen and up until 1813 a star replaced this dot alongside the factory mark. During the Marcolini period the factory struggled, especially during the Napoleonic Wars, for it no longer had a state subsidy to rely on. Meissen did, however, adapt to the new Classical taste, seen best in the fine figure modelling of Michel Victor Acier and Johann Carl Schonheit. Marcolini period examples are scarce, but during the nineteenth century their work enjoyed an extraordinary popularity. From 1814 new management instigated changes to restore the factory's reputation, tarnished by cheaper wares. Inferior products were abandoned and instead every piece of Meissen was decorated to high standards with the most careful attention to detail. Rivals claimed that this quality was only maintained by paying unreasonably low wages, but even so, Meissen was still expensive. Customers appreciated the workmanship, however, and its figures and vases sold in great numbers.

Writers used to refer to anything made after the Marcolini period as 'Late Meissen', a dismissive term ignoring the quality that nineteenth century pieces represent. The value of later Meissen porcelain has escalated over the past decade, however, and dealers now find nineteenth century Meissen far easier to sell than eighteenth century to new customers who want fine decorative ornaments. Only the best white Meissen porcelain went on to be painted. Anything substandard was cast aside, sold in an unfinished state to independent decorators such as the Wolfsohn workshop in Dresden. Meissen cancelled their marks on these faulty

goods by cutting a line through the middle of the crossed swords, and it is important to look out for this sign, as the new Hausmalers or outside decorators never took the same care over their enamelling and gilding, and some can be particularly crude.

While traditional models sold best, Meissen produced new designs to suit changes in fashion. Gothic and Renaissance tastes were met by the bulk purchase of moulds formerly used in glass factories. These produced fancy dishes with embossed modelling which was picked out in 'gloss gold', a bright gold lustre which tends to wear off over the years. Meissen supplied important export markets, especially in England and later in America and Australia. During the Art Nouveau period exciting productions were made, especially by a family of skilled chemists and painters named Hentschel, and curious figures by Paul Schurich. These are rarely seen today, for most customers preferred the old Dresden designs which continued to be made. The modern Meissen factory still produces many original Kändler figures and these are expensive, for Meissen refuses to compromise on quality. Compared to the cost of making these pieces today, old Meissen does not seem so expensive after all.

Because the crossed swords mark was widely copied, Meissen's system of workmen's marks provides a valuable aid to attribution. Tiny impressed numbers occur from the 1730s, and from the Marcolini period a painted number is usually present as well. Nineteenth century ornaments normally carry a mould number, often with a single letter prefix, incised (scratched into) the base. In the twentieth century these model numbers are generally impressed rather than incised.

Further reading

Dr Karl Berling, *Festive Publication to Commemorate the 200th Jubilee of... Meissen 1910* reprinted as *Meissen China, an Illustrated History,* 1972

Geoffrey Godden, *Guide to European Porcelain,* 1993

Hugo Morley Fletcher, *Meissen,* 1971

Otto Walcha, *Meissen Porcelain,* 1981

A Meissen rococo 'Seasons' clock case, 22½in. (57cm) high, re-issued c.1850. Many 18th century models proved far more popular in the 19th century, when quality was maintained at the highest levels.

investment, aided by the discovery of a new source of kaolin, provided a firm financial footing, and the mark of a shield, the *Bindenschild* taken from the arms of the Habsburgs, was now used. Wares follow Meissen closely but are often crude and poorly potted, especially those made for the Turkish market. Some fine painting was practised, however, and particularly good figures include the *Cris de Wien* series which at the time rivalled Meissen but are much less expensive today.

From 1783 an impressed code system was introduced, using the last digits of the year – 96 for 1796, 804 for 1804 and so on. These are a useful guide to dating, but cannot be totally trusted as decoration was often added later. The best period was from 1784-1805 when Konrad von Sorgenthal was director. Finely painted classical scenes, topographical views and flowers, on cabinet cups and display plates,

A Vienna teabowl and saucer from the du Paquier period. A Chinese shape but with very European decoration in Schwarzlot, *c.1730-40.*

2. VIENNA

The story of Viennese porcelain is not the simple chronology of a single factory. The first European rival to Meissen was established here in 1718 by Claudius du Paquier. Its close resemblance to early Böttger porcelain is hardly surprising as du Paquier relied on the knowledge of Samuel Stolzel, a defector from Meissen. After less than a year Stolzel returned to Meissen, taking with him the painter J.G. Herold, but not before he had established a tradition for fanciful *chinoiserie*. The other principal decoration at Vienna was *Schwarzlot* painting in black monochrome. Du Paquier porcelain is unmarked and hard to distinguish from Meissen. Even so, for a factory which survived until 1744, its products are surprisingly rare, evidence of a limited production and a commercial failure. In 1744, however, the works were taken over by the State. This

Joseph Nigg of Vienna is regarded by many as the finest china painter of all time. This 16½in. (42cm) high plaque of 1810 sold for £50,000 in 1994, and is truly a great work of art.

A selection of 18th century Vienna figures from the Dora Fischer collection. Surprisingly out of fashion today, Vienna figures fetch less than half as much as Meissen from the same period.

were framed with incredibly rich raised gilding and coloured grounds. The great flower painters Joseph Nigg and Joseph Fischer were responsible for magnificent plaques, exhibited as great works of art and deservedly so. These costly productions were subsidised by cheaper wares, but this inexpensive Vienna porcelain could not compete with smaller factories. During the 1850s Vienna was reduced to making exact copies of popular Meissen figures.

A massive 32in. (81.5cm) dish painted with 'The Triumph of Ariadne', by J. Wagner, an independent china decorator working for the retailer Ernst Wahliss in Vienna, c.1900. This is as fine as anything made at the old State factory.

The State factory's closure in 1864 was far from the end of the story. No further porcelain was made, but a large stock remained of substandard white porcelain, some of it seventy years old. This was sold off to the factory's best painters and gilders who, finding themselves out of work, set up on their own as independent decorators. Their work was accomplished, and they used authentic Vienna porcelain until the supply was exhausted. Thereafter blanks came from Dresden where the shield mark was added, for it was not felt to be wrong to copy the mark of a defunct manufactory. The best decorators were superb, especially the workshops of J. Wagner and Ernst Wahliss. The latter also ran a major china retail business and commenced the manu-facture of his own porcelain about 1895, having purchased many of the old State factory's moulds. Wahliss' Vienna porcelain is very fine, especially essays in the Art Nouveau taste. In the twentieth century the Augarten factory produced porcelain in Vienna, much of it of high quality, especially Secessionist designs of the 1920s. A great deal of late Vienna style porcelain is poor, however, using printed gold and litho-printed scenes, but some can still be highly decorative.

Further reading

Geoffrey Godden, *Guide to European Porcelain*, 1993

J.F. Hayward, *Vienna Porcelain of the du Paquier Period*, 1952

Neuwirth and Mrazek, *Wiener Porzellan*, 1970

The State factory at Berlin produced some amazing Art Nouveau porcelain such as this covered bowl, c.1900, although examples are rarely seen.

3. BERLIN

Wilhelm Kaspar Wegely commenced porcelain manufacture in Berlin in 1751, assisted by Johann Benckgraff who had worked alongside Ringler at Höchst. Delightful figures of Cupid were made, marked with the letter W, but the factory failed in 1757 and Wegely's porcelain is a great rarity today. Johann Gotzkowsky made a further attempt at porcelain in Berlin in 1761, but fared little better. After two years his bankrupt factory was sold to Frederick the Great. It thus became the Prussian State factory and the mark of a sceptre in underglaze blue was used.

Frederick was actively involved in the running of the Berlin factory and after the Seven Years War he brought experienced workers from Meissen to improve production. Frederick favoured a gentle version of rococo, with flowers and borders in pink or puce rather than an excessive use of gold. Scenes painted in monochrome can be particularly fine, and figures modelled by Franz Ferdinand Mayer were coloured in delicate pastel shades.

Nineteenth century Berlin is very different in style, with strong Classical and Biedermeyer

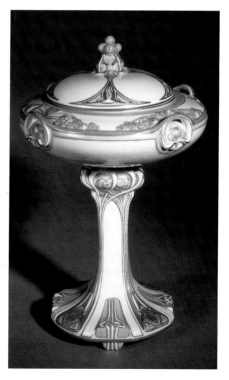

A superb example of Berlin topographical painting on a presentation plate showing the Palace of the Prince of Prussia, 9½in. (24.5cm), sceptre, orb and KPM marks, c.1870.

influences and wonderful gilding. The factory's speciality was *vedutenporzellan* with topographical views, mostly of Berlin, superbly painted on to cabaret sets, plaques and magnificent presentation vases commissioned by the State. Berlin is synonymous with magnificent porcelain plaques, but while some were painted at the factory, most were sold to independent decorators. These are further discussed on page 107. Lithophanes were another speciality and these wafer-thin panes of unglazed white porcelain, revealing detailed pictures when held to a bright light, are also known as Berlin Transparencies.

The initials KPM (for Konigliche Porzellan Manufactur) were used as a factory mark from about 1820. Other emblems used include the Prussian eagle and an orb. The sceptre mark in blue continued into the twentieth century. The Berlin factory declined late in the nineteenth century when many pieces were sold in white to Dresden decorators. Caution is needed, as pieces bearing sceptre marks were also made in Dresden and by Samson in Paris. Genuine Berlin examples made after 1870 can be distinguished by a diagonal stroke in the centre of the sceptre. An impressed date code was used starting with letter A for 1901, B for 1902 and so on. Greek letters were used from 1926. Although rarely seen, some of Berlin's best work dates from c.1900 when *Jugendstil*, the German equivalent of Art Nouveau, was used to great effect. The procession of figures modelled by Adolf Amberg for the wedding of the Crown Prince in 1905 is considered as a masterpiece of twentieth century sculpture. The Berlin factory was destroyed during World War II but a new works was constructed in the mid-1950s.

Further reading

Geoffrey Godden, *Guide to European Porcelain*, 1993

Margarete Jarchow, *Berlin Porcelain of the 20th Century*, 1988

A Frankenthal group of children playing with a dog, dated 1783, the colourful costumes reflecting the taste of the time, 9in. (23cm), Carl Theodor mark.

4. FRANKENTHAL

Paul-Anton Hannong first made porcelain in the French town of Strasbourg in 1752, aided by Joseph Ringler who had learn the secret knowledge at Vienna and Höchst. Due to Louis XV's injunction to protect the Vincennes manufactory (see page 69), Hannong moved the factory to Frankenthal in Germany in 1755. The initials PH or a lion painted in blue were used as marks by Paul Hannong and his two sons who continued the works until 1762 when financial difficulties forced the sale of the factory to the Elector Carl Theodor. His initials, CT below a crown, became the new mark painted in underglaze blue, and a simple dating system of the last two digits of the year was sometimes used, for example. 77 for 1777. Fine figure painting by Jakob Osterpey and others occurs on dramatic teasets and snuff boxes, but it is as a figure maker that Frankenthal is best known, thanks to the modelling of Konrad Linck, Karl Gottlieb Luck and especially Johann Peter Melchior who came from Höchst. Production declined during the 1780s and on the closure of the factory in 1799 some of the moulds were sold to Nymphenburg.

Further Reading
William Honey, *German Porcelain,* 1947
E. Pauls-Eisenbeiss, *German Porcelain of the Eighteenth Century,* 1972

Figures from the Italian Comedy by F.A. Bustelli, masterpieces of rococo re-issued in the creamy porcelain of the 1920s with bright colours inspired by the eighteenth century originals.
Private collection

5. NYMPHENBURG

Prince Maximilian Joseph of Bavaria commenced porcelain manufacture at Neudeck in 1747 using the skills of F.I. Niedermayer, but it was not until the arrival of Joseph Ringler in 1754 that any real success was achieved. The factory was moved to the royal palace at Nymphenburg in 1761. The very fine white porcelain body and delicate potting created exceptionally beautiful teawares and wonderful plates painted with flowers. A curious speciality was painted copies of black landscape prints pinned to a simulated wood ground known as *faux bois.* Nymphenburg is famous for its figures thanks to the genius of Franz Anton

Bustelli, a Swiss modeller who many regard as superior even to Kändler at Meissen. Bustelli's figures, including his remarkable Italian Comedy studies, capture rococo in the most dramatic fashion. These were usually sold just in white as pure sculpture. A few were originally coloured but a lot of the colouring found on Nymphenburg figures was added later. The factory mark was the shield of Bavaria, impressed into the white clay and often hard to see through the glaze. The factory declined after 1770 although there was a slight revival in 1799 when workmen including J.P. Melchior joined from the failed Frankenthal factory. A small production continued in the nineteenth century, principally cabinet wares and also very fine

Like most Höchst figures, these dancers are delicately modelled and full of charm, 4¾in. (12cm), c.1760.

plaques, but the factory struggled to compete with Berlin. The works were leased to a private company in 1862 and largely supplied Dresden decorators with white blanks. A revival in the twentieth century was due to the re-introduction of wonderful rococo figures based on original moulds. These are made of a soft creamy porcelain, quite different from the eighteenth century paste, although many collectors buy modern specimens thinking they have discovered a valuable original sculpture by Bustelli. High quality was maintained, however.

Further reading:
William Honey, *German Porcelain*, 1947
George Savage, *Eighteenth Century German Porcelain*, 1958

6. HÖCHST

Tradition tells us that Joseph Ringler, a painter at Vienna, learnt the secret of porcelain manufacture through an affair with du Paquier's daughter. Ringler arrived at an existing fayence factory at Höchst in 1751 and, together with Johann Benckgraff, introduced a fine white porcelain. Tablewares follow Meissen's lead and some fine painting was carried out, particularly in puce monochrome. Figures were a significant production, including fine models by Laurentius Russinger and Johann Peter Melchior. The colouring of Höchst figures is often distinctive, especially shaded grass bases and the use of dark brown spots to represent the eyes. The factory closed in about 1796 and its figure moulds were

A Ludwigsburg dinner plate, finely painted in the rococo taste, 9⅝in. (24.5cm), c.1765. Although the fine moulded border is filled with thick, creamy glaze, the quality still shines through.

ultimately sold to Müller's fayence works at Damm where the Höchst style was continued in pottery. Other later makers used Höchst moulds to create convincing porcelain fakes, in particular Dressel, Kister & Co. of Passau. The original factory mark, a wheel in enamel or blue, was an easy mark to copy.

A Furstenberg figure of a miner from a series modelled by Simon Feilner. The colouring typically dramatic, c.1770.

Further reading
William Honey, *German Porcelain*, 1947
E. Pauls-Eisenbeiss, *German Porcelain of the Eighteenth Century*, 1972

---

7. LUDWIGSBURG

After his numerous wanderings round Germany, Joseph Ringler finally arrived at Ludwigsburg in 1759 and was engaged by the Duke of Württemburg. Ringler remained here until he retired in 1802 but he rarely achieved the whiteness of his other porcelain ventures. Indeed, Ludwigsburg glaze often misfired to a grey-brown colour or became heavily smoked with dark specks. Accomplished modellers provided figures, including Johann Beyer and Jean Louis who, working under the designer

G.F. Riedel, modelled a delightful set of miniature figures of the stalls and sideshows at the annual Venetian Fair held in Württemburg. Another noteworthy series of figures depicted dancers of the Court ballet. Ludwigsburg tablewares are very much in Meissen style but generally of inferior quality. The mark of two letter Cs crossed below a crown was painted in underglaze blue and occasionally in enamel, but this can be confusing as the same device was also used in France at Niderviller. The porcelain made at Ludwigsburg declined appreciably from the 1780s although the works continued until 1824.

Further reading
E. Pauls-Eisenbeiss, *German Porcelain of the Eighteenth Century*, 1972

8. FURSTENBERG

The Duke of Brunswick, Carl I, experimented with porcelain with little success until Johann Benckgraff arrived from Höchst in 1753 bringing with him the modeller Simon Feilner. The latter was responsible for an exciting series of figures from the Italian Comedy and detailed studies of miners at work. The factory concentrated on useful wares, heavily moulded to hide imperfections, and the influence of Meissen is very much apparent. Some pieces do have an individuality, especially painted plaques and biscuit portrait busts and medallions inspired by Wedgwood. These continued into the nineteenth century when the factory survived largely on its past reputation. Feilner's figures were still produced, marked with the same cursive F in underglaze blue used a century before. Consequently, dating Furstenberg can be difficult. Meissen figures, vases and other ornaments were copied at Furstenberg and these frequently bear fake crossed swords marks. These can be distinguished by their snow white body, bright puce and gold edging and distinctive fanciful insects accompanying formal flower painting. Recent productions from Furstenberg are generally unoriginal.

Further reading
George Savage, *Eighteenth Century German Porcelain*, 1958

9. FULDA

One of the smallest German factories was established by Prince-Bishop Heinrich von Bibra at Fulda in 1764. By this date German porcelain was no longer a novelty and there was considerable competition, but by limiting the size of its production, Fulda was able to concentrate on quality. As a result the factory survived until 1789, making porcelain that has enormous appeal today, enhanced by its rarity. Fine figures included the work of Wenzel Neu and G. L. Bartoleme, and teawares are always delicate and carefully painted. The mark, FF below a crown, was much copied early in the twentieth century.

A single Fulda teacup painted with characteristic care, c.1775. Odd cups are often the only affordable way to collect examples of rare Continental factories.
Sandon collection

10. THURINGIA

This region of Germany was home to a considerable number of porcelain factories in the latter part of the eighteenth century. Their products have a similarity, for all aimed at the lower end of the market, copying Meissen and Berlin with all the rustic charm of Staffordshire copies of the great English porcelains. The principal Thuringian factories were Limbach, Gotha, Kloster Veilsdorf, Volkstedt and Wallendorf. Many productions were unmarked, and at different times the Greiner family managed seven different Thuringian factories. The Greiner's mark of a leaf-like trefoil was used by more than one factory, and Gotha and Gera both used the mark of a letter G. It is hardly surprising, therefore, that many figures and wares cannot be firmly identified beyond Thuringia.

Classical styles dominate Thuringian porcelain, reflecting largely the period when most were operating. Teawares mostly follow the same plain, cylindrical shapes and copy other German factory designs, especially with formal plant motifs either in puce or in underglaze blue. Some accomplished figures were made, including a fascinating series from the Italian Comedy modelled for Kloster Veilsdorf by Wenzel Neu who also worked at Fulda. Neu's work is valued highly, but a lot of Thuringian porcelain is inexpensive today relative to its rarity. In terms of quality this is

A Thuringian equestrian figure made at Wallendorf, typically clumsy and naïve, but quaint and not without charm, 7in. (18cm), c.1770-80.

not really surprising, but many pieces do have a simple charm, offering much scope to new collectors unable to afford Meissen figures from the eighteenth century.

Further Reading

Graul und Kurtzwelly, *Altthüringer Porzellan*

11. DRESDEN

The name most associated with German porcelain is not a maker at all but a style. Böttger invented porcelain in Augustus the Strong's castle in Dresden but the Royal Saxon Factory moved to Meissen around 1710. Its productions were known as Dresden throughout the

A typical Dresden vase decorated in the Wolfsohn workshop with a pattern copied from early Meissen, 13¾in. (35cm), AR mark, c.1870-80.

This model of an owl forms the base of an oil lamp, with glass eyes to create an eerie glow. Late 19th century Dresden porcelain, kitsch, maybe, but fun and decorative.

eighteenth and nineteenth centuries. Many other china factories, established in Germany in the nineteenth century, made copies of Meissen but, prevented from faking Meissen's crossed swords marks, they marketed their porcelain as 'Dresden Style'. Consequently most 'Dresden' was not made in the town of Dresden itself, but all over Germany.

The picture is complicated by independent porcelain decorators who set up in Dresden, painting copies of famous Meissen patterns on blanks bearing Meissen marks. Some decorators bought authentic Meissen white china 'seconds', readily available from the factory. To indicate the ware was substandard and thus not decorated at Meissen, the factory mark was cancelled with a line cut through the middle of the crossed

swords using a grinding wheel. Other decorators used porcelain made for them bearing fake Meissen marks. The best known of these was Helena Wolfsohn of Dresden who used porcelain marked with the legendary AR cipher of Augustus Rex, especially on cups and saucers and pairs of vases with coloured grounds and figure panels. Wolfsohn's porcelain is often known as 'Augustus Rex', for the AR mark was used for forty years from 1841. Meissen eventually won an injunction against Wolfsohn and from 1881 her workshop used a crown over the letter D instead. Other decorators made the same patterns, especially flowers on a white ground with lacy gold edges. The mark of the word Dresden and a crown (known as 'Crown Dresden') was used by several makers including

Three separate pieces of decorative Sitzendorf porcelain, inspired loosely by Meissen but aimed at quite a different market – well made, nevertheless. All marked in blue, 1880-1920.

the Klemm workshop. It is essential to watch for quality as some pieces can be disappointingly crude, while others, including the Lamm decorating workshop, made very high quality productions finished with rich raised gold (see page 86). Lamm's mark, understandably, was a drawing of a lamb.

For more than two centuries the name Dresden has been associated with china figurines – shepherds and shepherdesses, gallants and ladies and plump Cupids among dainty flowers. Dresden cherubs and modelled roses climb around mirror frames or support countless candelabra and table centrepieces. Groups of ladies taking tea, or dancing ballerinas, were adorned with fine lace made by dipping real lace into clay before firing. The ideas and most of the models originated at Meissen, but Dresden examples rarely approach the quality of the real Meissen factory. 'Dresden' figural ornaments were made all over Europe, including England, and are still made today, especially in the Far East. The best makers in this style are discussed under the entries for Sitzendorf, Plaue and Potschappel.

Further Reading

Geoffrey Godden, *Guide to European Porcelain*, 1993

12. SITZENDORF

The Voigt factory was established c.1840 in Sitzendorf, a long way from Dresden, but they made porcelain in the style much associated today with the generic term 'Dresden'. Sitzendorf porcelain was marked with two parallel lines crossed by a third line, a sign which could not be accused of copying Meissen's crossed swords, even though most Sitzendorf porcelain reproduced popular Meissen models. Putti or Cupids proliferate, but Voigt did not attempt to compete with Meissen quality or colouring, for a totally different palette of soft pastel colours was used. Encrusted flowers played a large part in Sitzendorf's production, especially roses in delicate pinks and yellows. These contributed to the factory's success, for their output between 1870 and 1910 was simply vast. Typical table centrepieces with basket tops are highly decorative and have popular appeal. As such they are not overtly expensive today. Later Sitzendorf productions are more colourful and the factory continues to the present. Twentieth century Sitzendorf is marked with the original crossed lines superimposed on a crowned letter S, sometimes with the word Dresden in addition.

A Plaue lithophane or 'Berlin Transparency',
lit from behind to make a detailed picture,
8¾in. x 6¾in. (22cm. x 17.5cm), impressed PPM
mark, c.1880. Plaue lithophanes are amongst
the best.

13. PLAUE

The Thuringian town of Plaue, or Plaue-am-
Havel, housed the large porcelain factory of
Schierholz & Sohn, established c.1820. Plaue
porcelain achieved fame only during the
second half of the nineteenth century for its
Dresden style ornaments and especially for its
lithophanes – thin slabs of unglazed white
porcelain which reveal a picture when held up to
a light. Also known as 'Berlin Transparencies',
lithophanes were made by the State factory in
Berlin, but Plaue examples are just as
accomplished and can form an interesting
collection. The mark PPM for Plaue Porzellan
Manufactur was neatly impressed in the
corners. From about 1875 Plaue produced a
vast number of very decorative ornaments in
the Meissen/Dresden style, especially pairs of

A traditional Dresden candelabra bearing the oak-
leaf mark of Plaue, c.1890 and good value as
decoration today.

candelabra and basket centrepieces applied
with figures and colourful flowers. These were
marked with two pairs of parallel lines crossed
at right angles, resembling a noughts and
crosses (tick-tack-toe) game, but be careful as
this mark also occurs on cheap printed
Bohemian porcelain. The later printed mark
used at Plaue was a crowned shield containing
three oak leaves.

German pierced plates are often called 'ribbon plates', but this Carl Thieme copy of Meissen, from a rich dessert set, is in a different class from the cheap printed wall plates, 7in. (18cm), c.1900.

Sandon collection

14. POTSCHAPPEL

In the town of Potschappel near Dresden, Carl Thieme ran a sizeable porcelain factory making decorative ornaments in the Meissen style. Some Potschappel vases stand over a metre (39in.) high and can be accomplished pieces of porcelain, heavily encrusted with china fruit and flowers painted in bright colours. Potschappel porcelain was widely exported, especially to Britain and the United States. The early period of the factory, from about 1870, used the painted mark of a cross with the letter T for Thieme. From about 1900 a printed mark combined an SP cipher with the word Dresden to denote the company's new trading name *Sachsische Porzellanfabrik*. This mark is still used today, especially on small figurines. In the nineteenth century blank Potschappel vases and cups and saucers were often decorated in the established Dresden workshops.

As an exercise in copying a master, a Berlin plaque of Rubens' boys on your wall is almost better than the real thing. This example is by Carl Meinhelt of Bamberg, 14½in. x 20½in. (36.5cm x 52cm), impressed KPM mark, c.1860.

'Die Neapolitaner', copied in glowing ceramic colours on a Berlin plaque, 9½in. x 7¼in. (24.5cm. x 18.5cm), impressed KPM, c.1870-80. A popular and highly commercial subject.

15. BERLIN AND OTHER PORCELAIN PLAQUES

Berlin made the best blank slabs of glazed porcelain and china painters across Europe appreciated these smooth and perfectly flat panels. Artists did not want their finest work spoilt by inferior porcelain and so they invested in more costly Berlin examples. Consequently, Berlin plaques were painted to a consistently high standard, whereas plaques by other makers are usually much inferior. Berlin plaques were exhibited in galleries as expensive works of art, and rightly so, for a good plaque involved a large number of kiln firings to build up gradually the colours and depth of detail. The artists were extremely skilled and proudly signed their own names on copies of famous paintings, for china painters were great copyists. Most could turn their hand to any subject, from solemn Rembrandts and Raphaels to voluptuous ladies by the contemporary artist Angelo Asti.

A typical example of Victorian humour, making fun of a visit to the dentist. Most fairings were made by Conta and Boehme.

Some plaque painters became famous, and names to watch for include Henry Bucker, Otto Wustlich, Carl Meinhelt, Carl Schmidt and R. Dittrich (who painted endless copies of the same painting of 'Ruth in the Cornfield'). Sadly, many plaques are not signed, and others can be confusing. The name Wagner occurs on plaques of greatly different competence, for at the Wagner family's china painting workshop in Vienna, different painters all 'signed' with the studio name of Wagner.

Berlin plaques were marked with the letters KPM and a sceptre impressed, usually at one end. Plaques were still made at Berlin in the 1930s and dating is difficult. The size of the plaque was occasionally scratched into the reverse, initially in inches but from the late nineteenth century centimetres were used. Superb plaques were also made at Nymphenburg, and at Meissen from the mid-nineteenth century. Ludwig Sturm had previously painted Berlin plaques and he introduced to Meissen the tradition of copying famous paintings. Vienna plaques are rare but

of exceptional quality, the finest painted by the great flower artist Joseph Nigg. Hutschenreuter was also a prolific maker of blank plaques, supplied to artists in Dresden and even in Rome. In Italy other plaques were made in Milan and Florence, mostly painted with Raphael's *Madonna del Sedia*. Some less expensive plaques were produced using lightly printed etchings as a guide to the painter and these delicate outlines can be difficult to detect. Recently fake Berlin plaques have been made in the Far East, using photographic techniques to copy valuable originals.

Further reading
Geoffrey Godden, *Guide to European Porcelain*, 1993

16. CONTA & BOEHME AND FAIRINGS

The saucy humour associated with seaside postcards can be traced back to German porcelain novelty figurines popular from the 1880s and '90s. The common title 'Fairings' derives from the long-held tradition that these were given as prizes at fairgrounds, but they were also sold in souvenir shops all over Britain. The titles are invariably in English, not German, for the customers were British holiday-makers at Margate, Blackpool and Worthing. Subjects range from the fairly innocuous 'Last into bed to put out the light', a reminder of the days of small houses where children shared a bed, to jokes on marriage, usually at the poor husband's expense. The humour is lavatorial at the level which school-children might find amusing today. Fairings were keenly collected in the 1960s and '70s but the market has not kept pace and they can be very reasonably priced now. Many fairings are marked with an impressed shield with an arm holding a sword, the emblem used by the firm of Conta & Boehme of Possneck in Saxony. This prolific maker also produced an extensive range of cheap and cheerful, untitled china ornaments which they marketed at the time as 'Bazaar goods in all price ranges'. These are rarely expensive and can form a decorative collection.

This Rudolstadt table centrepiece from the Art Nouveau period of c.1900 may lack the skill of a master potter, but its decorative value is not debased, 16in. (41cm) high.

Further reading
Margaret Anderson, *Victorian Fairings and their Values*, 1975

17. RUDOLSTADT AND VOLKSTEDT

Porcelain making in Thuringia goes back to the eighteenth century (see page 101), but one hundred years later many new factories were operating here producing decorative figurines and ornaments. The important towns of Rudolstadt and Volkstedt were home to many manufacturers. Thuringian porcelain mostly follows Dresden traditions, while a particular speciality of Rudolstadt was the copying of the matt ivory finish of Royal Worcester. A great deal of Rudolstadt porcelain was sold in Britain and America, especially in the Japanesque style. The firm of Lewis Straus & Sons registered the name of 'The New York and Rudolstadt Pottery Company' in order, it is said, to avoid paying duty on importation to America, but they did have a large wholesale outlet in New York. Straus believed in

deception, for their mark was the letters RW in a crowned diamond, used with the clear intent of fooling customers into thinking their ornaments were made by Royal Worcester. One neglected Rudolstadt maker, Ernst Bohne & Sohne, produced inexpensive but very pretty figurines, glazed or in bisque, which are basic but well made. The firm was established c.1854 and from 1878 used the mark of an anchor in blue with the initials EB either side. The impressed letters EBS were also used. Delightful small models of animals or little chinamen were made in matt ivory to simulate oriental netsukes. Bohne of Rudolstadt is well worth collecting, for its work is not expensive.

The old Volkstedt mark of one or two pitchforks was originally designed to imitate Meissen, but by the late nineteenth century this was an established sign, used by several makers in Volkstedt. Many Dresden style figures were made here, and a range of table centrepieces copy the Art Nouveau style of Royal Dux and Ernst Wahliss of Vienna.

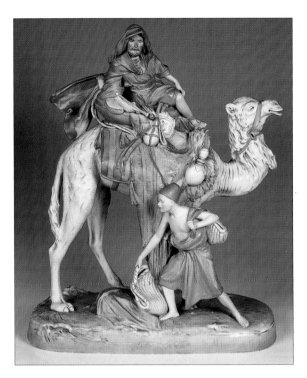

The colouring copies Royal Worcester, the model copies Austrian painted bronze. Together this is classic Royal Dux, and magnificent too.

Volkstedt examples are usually well modelled and were made in a particularly thin cast porcelain which has a pleasant lightness. The firm of Eckert & Co. made a large number of delicate figurines and groups, while the Aelteste Volkstedter Porzellanfabrik produced impressive large figure groups adorned with lace. These are usually marked with an elaborate crowned cipher resembling the old mark of Fulda, Most are sold as Dresden today and the names of the principal Thuringian factories are largely ignored.

Further reading
Geoffrey Godden, *Guide to European Porcelain*, 1993

18. ROYAL DUX

The porcelain factory at Dux (or Duchcov) in Bohemia achieved notoriety for its copies of Royal Worcester, but to condemn it merely as a copyist is a gross simplification. Its name was an attempt to fool the British public, for it had no tradition of royal patronage, Also the matt ivory and bronze finish used by Royal Dux was undoubtedly inspired by Royal Worcester; but Dux never copied actual Worcester figures. Instead the designs came from bronzes, particularly the cold-painted bronzes from Austria. Farm workers and Eastern tribesmen are not dissimilar to Royal Worcester, but it is in the area of Art Nouveau sculpture that Royal Dux excelled, producing original models with grace and movement all of their own. A raised pink triangle mark impressed 'Royal Dux. Bohemia' was applied to the bases. From 1920 Dux became part of Czechoslovakia but the name Bohemia was still used, so do not assume pieces marked Bohemia were made before 1920. Traditional Dux models continued but the quality declined and some were made in

Two identical R.S. Prussia plates, early 20th century. Single plates can be mistaken for hand painting, but together it is clear a photo-litho printing technique was used.

cheaper pottery. However, during the 1930s a range of exciting new Art Deco figures were made, in creamy-white, blue and gold, and these are stylish and keenly collected. The original factory had been founded by Edward Eichler and the initial E occurs in the centre of the triangle marks. After World War II this was changed to a D for Dux and to an M from c.1953. Although it struggled, the factory survived and still makes a wide range of models based on earlier productions, marked with the same pink triangle. Care needs to be taken as modern Dux porcelain is imported in quantity into Britain and regularly turns up in provincial auctions where it is mistaken for old.

19. RS PRUSSIA

The firm of Reinhold Schlegelmilch is better known by its initials and place name used as a factory mark from about 1880. The company had factories at Suhl and also at Tillowitz and these names sometimes replace Prussia on the mark which was usually printed in more than one colour on thin, almost eggshell porcelain. RS Prussia is famous for its delicate shaded decoration produced by combining aerograph spray and photographic-litho technology. The quality of RS Prussia's colour printing is exceptionally fine and it is quite wrong to condemn these pieces as examples of cheap printing. Decoration is mostly floral but copies of famous paintings and attractive portraits or animals are occasionally to be found. The fame and surprising high values associated with RS Prussia china is due to its original success in the United States, where there are today a large number of collectors. Indeed, it is not unknown for rare examples to command several thousand dollars a piece. Later examples after 1920 were marked RS Germany or RS Poland, on pieces made for the British market in the last years of the factory.

Further reading

Clifford Schlegelmilch, *RS Prussia,* 1970

CHAPTER 11

ENGLAND

INTRODUCTION

Although the eighteenth century Kings of England used fine foreign porcelain, they showed no desire to invest in a state porcelain factory. As a result porcelain making in England relied on private enterprise with no princely subsidy as a cushion against failure. Meissen, Sèvres and Capodimonte, for example, could concentrate on quality, whereas English factories had to focus on profit. The English had to make what their customers wanted at a competitive price, for Chinese porcelain was readily available in England and wealthy customers could afford to pick and choose. English factories either copied Chinese to undercut the oriental imports, or reproduced scarce kinds of porcelain. French and German porcelain was not available openly in England in the mid-eighteenth century, but there was plenty to be borrowed from private collections acquired abroad. Japanese porcelain had not been imported since the 1730s, and the old Chinese white porcelain from Dehua had not been seen for fifty years. Consequently these were now collector's items, and there was a keen second-hand market in Kakiemon and *blanc de chine*. Different factories copied Meissen, Japan and China among other areas where it was felt

An early Worcester teabowl and saucer, not a direct copy, but heavily inspired by the Chinese porcelain customers were already used to in 1752.

there would be a profitable demand for English-made porcelain.

Successful businessmen who wanted to invest in the manufacture of porcelain looked to scientists and alchemists who claimed to have perfected the secret processes. All early makers were hindered by a lack of kaolin, as the so-called 'china clay' had not yet been discovered in Cornwall. 'True' or hard paste porcelain required kaolin and, to compensate, English factories tried various substitutes – white clay, glass, and especially calcined animal bones. They also used a special stone from Cornwall known as soaprock. Porcelain containing a high proportion of animal bone is known as 'phosphatic', while that made with soaprock is called 'steatitic'. Various secret formulae, closely guarded by the factories, resulted in differences in appearance from one firm to another. This is vital, as very little early English porcelain is marked in any way.

Many factories copied each other as the market for English porcelain grew in the 1770s. Worcester dominated the scene with durable and elegant teawares, while Derby, whose body could not withstand use with hot tea, replaced Bow as the principal figure maker. True porcelain, using Cornish kaolin, was attempted at Plymouth and Bristol with only moderate

A Bow figure of a saltbox player, copied from Meissen but executed in a down-to-earth English manner, 5in. (12.5cm), c.1752.

Rustic Staffordshire lions, c.1840, not in pottery but cast in a bone china body. Attributed to John and Rebecca Lloyd but the maker hardly matters. 4¾in. (12cm).

Imitations of old stained ivory, a speciality of Royal Worcester that epitomises the taste of the 1890s.

commercial success, but the patent used by Richard Champion at Bristol led eventually to New Hall and other Staffordshire factories' 'hybrid' hard-paste recipes. The hybrid body was easy to make and hard-wearing, and was understandably popular.

Cheap Chinese and French imports, along with economic recession saw the demise of many English porcelain makers by the 1790s. Those who survived either aimed at the mass market with inexpensive teawares, or targeted the nobility with high quality goods – the best that money could buy. Derby and Worcester abandoned everyday tablewares and focused on fine porcelain, always finished with the very best gold. New markets opened and Staffordshire factories found they also could sell tea and dessert services in the rich Regency taste. Spode introduced bone china, a new kind

of body which revolutionised the industry in Britain. Heavy competition meant British factories were fighting for a share in the same market. All made similar teawares, vases and figurines in the latest flamboyant taste. In the 1830s, as France gave way to Dresden as the principal influence, Derby and Worcester were slow to adapt and lost ground to Staffordshire and Coalport. Factories came and went, including the superb Welsh porcelain of Swansea and Nantgarw and the eccentric Rockingham works in Yorkshire. On the other hand, by aiming at different ends of the market, many enterprising firms prospered. The Staffordshire makers Davenport, Ridgway, Minton and Spode/Copeland, together with Coalport and the Worcester factories, accounted for an incredible output of fine ornamental porcelain as well as everyday

Every major factory is famous for one kind of porcelain above any other, in this case Wedgwood's 'Fairyland Lustre' and Minton's pâte-sur-pâte, *these vases by Alboin Birks, 7¾in. (20cm).*

tablewares. Their success depended on the ability to follow fashion and produce porcelain in the latest style – from rococo to Mediaeval and Gothic and on to High-Victorian Renaissance. Parian was a major discovery and revolutionised figure making in the 1850s and '60s. The reopening of Japan created a sensation and Minton and Royal Worcester took it to heart. During the 1870s Japanesque porcelain accounted for a substantial part of their output.

England now led Europe in artistic porcelain but somehow the momentum was lost as the spirit of Art Nouveau swept the Continent. English pottery makers followed the French and Austrian leads but the porcelain factories in England made only half-hearted attempts at Art Nouveau and Art Deco designs. Instead, most English porcelain of the twentieth century harks back to the past. Royal Worcester and Royal Crown Derby continued to make Victorian shapes and designs, often superbly painted by artists who were now permitted to sign their work. Mass-produced imports from Germany had a serious effect on the cheaper end of the British porcelain trade. During the First World War, English makers were encour-

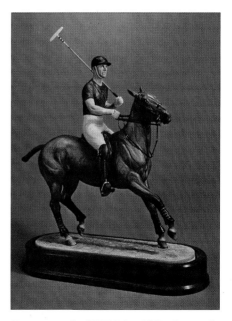

Equestrian study of HRH Prince Philip playing polo, modelled by Doris Lindner and produced by Royal Worcester as a limited edition.

A Dehua blanc-de-chine beaker, transformed by exciting English painting, probably c.1748-50, 2½in. (6.5cm). Sandon collection

A figure of Guanyin, copied from Chinese white porcelain but bearing the raised anchor mark of Chelsea, 4¾in. (12cm), c.1750.

aged to produce figurines in order to recapture the market in cheap ornaments. During the 1920s Royal Doulton greatly expanded their popular range of pretty china figures, followed in the 1930s by Royal Worcester and others. A buoyant trade in 'Limited Editions' in the 1960s and '70s saw the creation of many stunning porcelain sculptures although a collectors' market has yet to materialise.

1. CHINESE PORCELAIN ENAMELLED IN ENGLAND

References to 'China Painters' working in England as early as 1729 fascinated collectors who looked for evidence of porcelain making prior to the establishment of the Chelsea factory. In reality, the only porcelain available to such painters was Chinese. Plain white Chinese wares were brought back in trading ships, mostly to Holland where there had been a long tradition of china painting. While most of the European painting found on Chinese porcelain was added in Holland, enamellers did work in Germany and England too. Painting closely resembling that of Chelsea, can be ascribed to London decorators and

research by Dr Bernard Watney has identified a considerable number of different hands. The best known was James Giles who came from a family of china painters and dealers in porcelain, working first at Kentish Town and then in Soho. Distinctive fancy birds and landscapes in green monochrome can be linked to the Giles workshop. Other rare Chinese pieces can be ascribed to the hand of the Chelsea artist Jefferyes Hamett O'Neale, and a curious group of Chinese pieces occur with overglaze transfer prints, some from engravings by Robert Hancock. Once English porcelain became established, and Worcester in particular, the independent enamellers no longer bothered with Chinese blanks, apart from gilding added to Chinese blue and white later in the eighteenth century.

Further reading

Geoffrey Godden, *Oriental Export Market Porcelain*, 1979

2. CHELSEA

Early Chelsea porcelain is incredibly beautiful, with a thick, glassy glaze resembling the silkiness of Vincennes. Nicholas Sprimont, the owner of the Chelsea factory, was an important silversmith who moved in the same artistic circles as painters and sculptors including Hogarth and Roubiliac. Rococo dominated London taste in the 1740s and Sprimont's silver shapes transformed brilliantly into white Chelsea porcelain. A shrewd businessman, Sprimont knew his porcelain would be more costly than the plentiful Chinese export wares, so instead of copying Chinese, Chelsea set out to reproduce special porcelain not available in England. Collectors were paying high prices for Chinese *blanc de chine* figures and Japanese Kakiemon which had not been imported for many years. Also trade restrictions and the Seven Years War prevented the sale of Meissen and Vincennes porcelain in England. Chelsea copied these collectors pieces and created new designs in the European taste.

The chronology of Chelsea divides into periods determined by the form of factory mark. The Triangle period (c.1744-49) is famed for its silver shapes in plain white or with restrained colouring, occasionally marked with a triangle scratched into the base, or very rarely with a trident painted in blue. During the Raised Anchor period (c.1749-52) a mark of a tiny anchor embossed on an oval pad of clay was used on some pieces. Principal influences at this time were old Japanese Kakiemon, and Vincennes. Beautiful landscape painting and delightful fable subjects were introduced, some by the Irish artist Jefferyes Hamett O'Neale who gave his animals wonderful human expressions. Meissen was the important influence during the Red Anchor period (c.1752-56), when the factory mark was painted in red enamel, always small and usually tucked out of sight by the footrim or at the back of a figure model. German flower and

Porcelain birds had become popular at Meissen and Chelsea found a ready market in London for well-loved English species. 6in. (15.5cm), c.1752.

bird painting was carefully copied, and Sir Charles Hanbury Williams lent his collection of Meissen figures to be reproduced at Chelsea along with the style of colouring. Other original figures were produced, some modelled by Joseph Willems. Botanical painting was an important new decoration, unique to Chelsea, copied from flower prints and known after Sir Hans Sloane, the eminent botanist.

Chelsea discovered a beautiful new decoration when botanical flower prints were first available in London. 8½in. (21.5cm), Red Anchor period, c.1756.

The Gold Anchor period (c.1756-1769) saw a significant change in direction with the influence of Sèvres porcelain. While the factory mark changed to an anchor in gold, the Red Anchor mark was still used on some Meissen style products, while a class of inferior wares in traditional style, often without gilding, was marked with a brown anchor. These marks now appear in the middle of the bases and are larger in size. The new fashion was for coloured grounds, especially deep blue, known as mazarine, and a splendid claret. Gilding was widely used and rococo shapes became more eccentric. Figures were placed on fancy scroll bases with masses of modelled flowers forming bocage. In spite of good modelling and painting, the quality of Chelsea's potting deteriorated in the Gold Anchor period. The thick, dribbling glaze tended to craze heavily, resulting in unsightly staining. This led to the closure of the factory in 1769, although this was blamed on Sprimont's ill health. The works were bought by William Duesbury, who continued production at

Chelsea in conjunction with his own Derby factory until 1784, trading as Duesbury & Co. The wares made at this time are today known as Chelsea-Derby. The problem of poor glazing was resolved, and rococo was replaced by the new fashion for classical designs which were perfectly understood. The Gold Anchor mark was still used, along with a combined anchor and D in gold, as well as a crowned letter D usually in blue enamel.

Chelsea is the most widely copied of all English factories. Figurines marked with red or gold anchors have been made in vast numbers in Germany and France, so instead of trusting the marks alone, it is essential to look for other distinctive clues to aid identification. At Chelsea pieces were supported in the kiln on pointed clay trivets that left three 'stilt marks' where the little peg supports were snapped off. Dribbling glaze left uneven bases and footrims that needed to be ground down on a grindstone to make them lie flat. Other Chelsea bases were unglazed. Look out for puddles and droplets of thick glaze caught in crevices in a figure group or hanging from limbs or branches. Also watch for 'moons', tiny bubbles of air trapped in the porcelain which show up as lighter spots when a strong lamp is shone through a piece of Chelsea. Finally, while early Chelsea rarities command very high sums, it is worth remembering that Chelsea is generally still plentiful and some interesting examples, especially from the Gold Anchor period, can be acquired for quite reasonable prices.

Further reading

Elizabeth Adams, *Chelsea Porcelain,* 1987
John Austin, *Chelsea Porcelain at Williamsburg,* 1977
Margaret Legge, *Flowers and Fables,* National Gallery of Victoria, 1984

A Limehouse serving dish, c.1746-48, carefully painted and an unusually large example of this experimental porcelain. 8½in. (22cm) wide.

3. LIMEHOUSE

London newspaper advertisements for the 'New Invented Limehouse Ware' began a search for blue and white porcelain made in East London in the mid-1740s. Research showed that a china factory had been established at Duke Shore in Limehouse by Joseph Wilson & Co. It operated only briefly, from 1746-48, making blue and white generally in the Chinese style, but using shapes derived from English silver. In 1989 archaeologists from the Museum of London excavated the site and found shards confirming a class of porcelain, previously attributed to Liverpool, was in reality the missing Limehouse Ware. Limehouse specialised in sauceboats and pickle dishes, in great variety. Ambitious tureens were also attempted, as well as serving dishes,

octagonal teapots and a model of a seated cat. The shapes are exciting and the blue painting generally careful in a mix of Chinese and European styles. Severe firing problems led to the failure of the factory, for many of the surviving Limehouse pieces are misshapen or unevenly glazed. Following bankruptcy in 1748, the partners responsible for Limehouse remained active in the business, one moving to Staffordshire, another probably establishing the Bristol factory the following year. A very small amount of coloured Limehouse is known and it is believed the enamelling was executed in Holland.

Further reading
Limehouse Ware Revealed, English Ceramic Circle, 1993

A silver-shaped sauceboat decorated with so-called 'polychrome printing', a process unique to the Vauxhall factory. c.1756.

4. VAUXHALL

Many English porcelain ventures resulted from partnerships between practical potters and artistic entrepreneurs. Nicholas Crisp, a jeweller and founder of the Society of Arts, joined John Sanders at the latter's delftware pottery near Lambeth in South London. Crisp must have dreamt of the success afforded Chelsea and Bow, and hoped that his soaprock formula, not too different from that of Worcester, would bring him fortunes, but sadly he misunderstood his market. Blue and white Vauxhall teawares, painted in a delft-like manner, copied Chinese just as Bow had done, but in the mid-1750s real Chinese was probably cheaper. Like Bow, Vauxhall looked instead to figure making, but Crisp's modeller, John Bacon, was not really good enough and very few must have sold. Some enamelled Vauxhall porcelain is very beautiful, especially flower-painted vases and snuff boxes, and a curious rarity is the use of 'polychrome printing' overglaze, filling engravings with more than one colour before transferring the image. A fair amount of Vauxhall porcelain was made between the approximate dates of 1752 and 1763 when Crisp was bankrupt, but none was recognised until the site of the factory was excavated in 1988

by the Museum of London. The distinctive bright tone of blue painting and slightly iridescent glaze – known to collectors as 'sticky blue' – had until this time been incorrectly attributed to the Liverpool maker William Ball. No factory mark was used at Vauxhall.

Further reading

Bevis Hillier, *Early English Porcelain,* 1992
Bernard Watney, *English Blue and White Porcelain,* revised 1973

5. BOW

Bow's claim to be the biggest porcelain factory in England was no idle boast, but its beginnings were humble. The works were situated in Essex at Stratford-le-Bow, to the East of London, not to be confused with the Bow in the City of London. Unlike the earliest products of Chelsea and Worcester, the few pieces of Bow that can be dated to the first five years of the factory are coarse and decidedly experimental. Bow's formula relied on an imported clay from America, introduced by Andrew Duché who is believed to have attempted porcelain manufacture in Georgia in the 1730s. Edward Heylyn, a potter and glass maker, and Thomas Frye, an artist and engraver, were granted their first

Bow's interpretation of rococo is full of charm, partly due to the naïve modelling of John Toulouse. Some of these ornaments bear his T mark, c.1758-65.

patent in 1744, but it was not until 1748, when Frye alone took out a new patent, that any success can be claimed. Frye's important contribution to English porcelain was the addition of burnt animal bone as a strengthening agent, the main ingredient ultimately in bone china. Bow's 'phosphatic' paste lacks the delicacy and translucence of Worcester or indeed Chinese porcelain, but it could be produced cheaply and as a result Bow found a ready market for its copies of Oriental imports. Apart from shapes such as sauceboats and shell pickle stands derived from English silver, the bulk of Bow's tableware during the 1750s was copied from China and Japan. A series of Bow inkwells inscribed 'Made at New Canton 1750' emphasise the factory's intent on copying the porcelain of the East, and the new Bow factory premises were even built to look like the warehouses in Canton. White sprigged porcelain after Dehua *blanc-de-chine,* and painted patterns in kakiemon style sold well because the originals were no longer imported, but *famille*

rose plates and blue and white teawares reproduced contemporary Chinese porcelain.

Bow's underfired paste tended to stain brown and was not as durable as Worcester's soaprock body. As a result Worcester nearly monopolised English teawares, forcing Bow to look to a new market in porcelain figures copying the Dresden (or Meissen) taste. Meissen and Bow were truly worlds apart, for Bow models combine German elegance with the coarse naïvety of Staffordshire pottery figures – understandable as Bow is known to have engaged workmen from Staffordshire. As fashions changed, Bow figures become more complex, the simple mound bases of the 1750s replaced by fancy rococo scroll bases and modelled bocage in the 1760s. The colouring used on Bow figures is very distinctive, in particular bright puce and thick opaque turquoise enamels.

Thomas Frye retired in 1759, dying three years later. The Bow factory continued until the mid-1770s, supplying the same market in England with copies of the popular products of its rivals Chelsea, Derby and Worcester, but with little that was innovative. Today Bow is generally far less expensive than other English porcelain and this is perfectly understandable. There are, however, enormous opportunities for collectors, as the very best Bow has a unique beauty and only rarities command the kind of prices they deserve.

Apart from workmen's symbols, single letters and numerals, Bow did not use factory marks, the only exception being the sign of an anchor and dagger side by side in red enamel. This was used c.1765-75 on brightly coloured porcelain in London taste and it is likely there was some connection between Bow and the decorating studio of James Giles in Kentish Town.

Further reading

Elizabeth Adams and David Redstone, *Bow Porcelain,* 1981

Peter Bradshaw, *Bow Porcelain Figures,* 1992

Anton Gabszewicz and Geoffrey Freeman, *Bow Porcelain, the Freeman Collection,* 1982

---

6. ST. JAMES'S

The mystery of the 'Girl-in-a-Swing' class of early English porcelain was finally solved in 1993 with the publication of a paper by Bernard Dragesco detailing documents in French archives. It had been known that the London jeweller Charles Gouyn was connected with a 'Chelsea China Warehouse' in St. James's, but it is now clear the St. James's porcelain was a totally separate enterprise to Nicholas Sprimont's Chelsea factory, and Sprimont himself issued newspaper advertisements in 1749 and 1751 to dissociate himself from Gouyn. The factory at Gouyn's house in Bennet Street, St. James's was small, specialising in the production of 'Toys'. The term was used at the time to refer to small porcelain novelties, principally scent bottles, seals and bonbonnières. Similar objects were made in France and Germany and the Chelsea factory produced a wide range of toys. St. James's toys can be distinguished from Chelsea by their naïve modelling and primitive

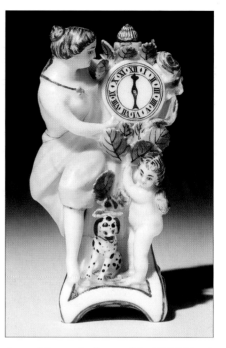

A porcelain scent bottle, one of the delightful 'toys' which were the speciality of the St. James factory, 2¾in. (7cm), c.1755.

painting, but they are charming none the less and Gouyn's background as a jeweller is reflected in the quality of the gold mounts with which they were sold. It seems likely that the St. James's factory operated from 1749-59. Before it was correctly identified, the factory was referred to as 'Girl-in-a-Swing', named after an important figure group in the Victoria and Albert Museum. The factory made a number of figures, many of which have the same quaint modelled faces and large applied leaves found on scent bottles. Teawares made at the St. James's factory, with distinctive flower painting, are amongst the rarest of all eighteenth century porcelains.

Further reading

Bernard Dragesco, *English Ceramics in French Archives,* 1993

A covered bowl for strawberries on a lively rococo base, made at Derby c.1757. Rare and exciting.

7. DERBY

The early history of Derby porcelain falls into distinct phases, but, unlike Chelsea, there are no changing factory marks to help historians differentiate between the periods. The story began in Derby probably in 1748 with the arrival of Andrew Planché. A Huguenot like Nicholas Sprimont, Planché had trained as a jeweller in London but had also probably gained experience visiting French porcelain factories. The earliest recognised Derby – white cream jugs dated

1750 – are very similar to Triangle period Chelsea, although Derby's glassy paste is creamier. Some writers have confused Andrew Planché with Andrew Duché who had supplied American clay for the Bow factory and may have been involved with William Cookworthy during the 1740s. It has been suggested that Planché was not involved with the Derby factory at all, but surviving evidence very much favours Planché as the modeller of some exciting early Derby figures in Chinoiserie taste, and not the mysterious Duché.

A pair of Derby 'Mansion House Dwarfs', c.1810. Such figures were known as grotesques *but were popular because they were fun.*

The so-called 'Dry Edge' period which followed is named after the firing method which involved wiping the glaze away from the edge of the bases of porcelain models to prevent them adhering to the kiln shelf. The change in appearance of the paste, which became whiter and chalkier, was probably due to William Duesbury, a London china painter and retailer who had been at Longton Hall. Together with John Heath, Duesbury joined Planché at Derby in 1756. It appears Planché left Derby soon afterwards and possibly worked at Chelsea in 1758. Knowing so well the London market, Duesbury chose not to compete with Worcester's teawares, as Derby's body was prone to cracking with hot liquids. Instead in early Derby we find mostly ornamental shapes – baskets for fruit, butter

tubs, dessert dishes, cream pots and novelty tureens. Distinctive bird and flower painting was attributed by early collectors to a 'Moth Painter' and a 'Cotton Stem Painter', but clearly many artists followed the factory style.

Derby achieved fame as England's foremost figure maker. The earliest examples include some of the most exciting – Chinoiserie groups with a great sense of movement, theatrical studies of actors posing, and animals with a sculptural quality. These were usually left in the white and certainly work better without colouring. Figures from the mid-1750s have been called the 'Pale Family' because of the soft palette of enamels favoured by Duesbury and Heath. From about 1758 the factory grew in size and prosperity on the success of its figure making as popular models sold in great

A sumptuous Derby plate, combining fine botanical painting with high quality gilding, c.1810.

numbers. These include shepherds and shepherdesses, the so-called 'Ranelagh Dancers' and many mythological subjects. No wonder contemporary accounts refer to Derby as 'The Second Dresden'. Derby modelling is sharper than Bow, and the colouring is much more subtle. Derby figures, and most wares also, were supported in the kiln on balls of clay which left marks on the base where they had been attached. These 'pad marks' or 'patch marks' are a definite clue to a Derby origin, although similar firing methods were practised elsewhere, especially at Longton Hall.

In 1770 William Duesbury and his partner bought the Chelsea factory and also, in the mid-1770s, acquired what remained of the Bow and Vauxhall works. Chelsea's use of bone ash was combined with Derby's superior potting skills so

that Chelsea-Derby teawares were a considerable improvement. Duesbury & Co. continued production at Chelsea until 1784 and the Gold Anchor mark was still used, sometimes combined with a letter D in gold. A new mark of a crowned D in blue enamel was the mark principally used at Derby. Neo-classical decoration dominated, especially in green monochrome (see page 32) or with careful gilding combined with deep blue borders in an overglaze enamel known as 'Smith's Blue'. Figures continued to reflect rococo, with a refreshing Continental influence introduced by new modellers from Tournai. Other figures were converted to the classical fashion by the addition of new style bases. Particularly fine figures were made in unglazed white biscuit, very delicate and always of the highest quality.

William Duesbury II took over the factory on his father's death in 1786. Figures remained important, but the emphasis of the factory moved towards 'cabinet wares'. Dessert services were made for showing off, while vases and cups and saucers were placed on expensive furniture as elegant decoration, for these were too costly to use for drinking out of. Derby learnt from the mistakes of others and chose not to compete with cheaper Staffordshire teasets. Instead fine artists painted the thin, creamy porcelain and the best gilding framed their miniature masterpieces. Painters such as landscape specialist Zachariah Boreman learnt their skills at the factory, while other artists such as fruit painter George Complin had trained as a miniaturist and enameller. Derby's most famous artist, William Billingsley, produced his best flower painting at Derby in the 1780s before leaving for Pinxton in 1796. The late eighteenth century Derby factory mark was a crown, crossed batons and dots, and letter D, neatly painted in blue or purple.

Duesbury II died in 1797 and with him ended Derby's Golden Age. The factory continued under the control of his widow Elizabeth who married her husbands' former partner, Michael Kean. Then in 1811 the factory was bought by the company's clerk, Robert Bloor who remained in control until a mental breakdown in 1828. The factory mark changed in colour to red around 1800, and the lack of care with which the mark was now painted reflects the great changes that had occurred as Derby faced intense competition from Worcester, Coalport and Staffordshire. The quality of Derby's body gradually declined, and from c.1820 the paste is prone to severe crazing and staining. At this time the factory specialised in dinner and tea services painted in the bright 'Japan' patterns for which Derby is famous. Other cheap sets served to malign the factory's reputation, but some fine decoration continued on ornamental porcelain during the nineteenth century, including pots of modelled flowers and finely painted plaques. During Robert Bloor's illness the works were managed by James Thomason but the Bloor name was continued with badly-printed 'Bloor Derby' marks. Figure making remained important, and a new influence from Meissen is particularly noticeable around 1830. The marks of Meissen and Sèvres were copied in an attempt to revive Derby's reputation, but competition from Staffordshire and pottery figures in particular affected Derby's fortunes. The works eventually closed down in 1848.

Further reading

H. Gilbert Bradley (Ed.), *Ceramics of Derbyshire*, 1978

Peter Bradshaw, *Derby Porcelain Figures*

John Twitchett, *Derby Porcelain*, 1980

8. BRISTOL PORCELAIN MANUFACTORY (MILLER AND LUND)

Dr Richard Pocock, writing of a visit to the Bristol premises, stated that it was established by 'one of the principal manufacturers at Limehouse which failed'. Clearly there was a direct link with the porcelain made at

A Lund's mug, c.1750. The opaque dribbled glaze and other kiln imperfections reveal this as the product of a factory in its infancy, and thus a collector's joy.

Limehouse up until 1748, although the partners in the Bristol works – a copper merchant William Miller and a grocer and banker, Benjamin Lund – are not yet known to have been directly connected with the Limehouse venture. Lund was granted a licence to mine soaprock in Cornwall in March 1749, and this was a vital ingredient in the Bristol porcelain. Simple blue and white teawares copied Chinese and, as at Limehouse, these are unmarked. Bristol felt proud enough, however, to mark its name in raised letters on the bottom of embossed sauceboats and creamboats which were based on English silver shapes. While Limehouse attempted European subjects on some of their products, Bristol's blue painting followed only Chinese designs, the simple scenes or flowers appearing hazy beneath the thick glaze clouded by tiny bubbles. Fine spreading mugs show the Bristol body could stand up reasonably well in the firing. After barely two years of only modest success, the Bristol porcelain factory was acquired by partners in the ailing Worcester business and all 'stock and utensils and effects' were transferred to Worcester during 1752. Benjamin Lund moved to Worcester also where his primitive soaprock formula was perfected into the most successful of all English porcelains.

Further reading
John Sandon, *Dictionary of Worcester Porcelain,*
 ACC, 1993
Bernard Watney, *English Blue and White Porcelain,* revised 1973

A vase from the first year of production at Worcester, c.1752, combining gentle Chinese style enamelling with a unique and powerful shape. 12¼in. (31.25cm). Sold for £30,000 in June 1996.

---

9. WORCESTER

Of the English factories established in the mid-eighteenth century, Worcester alone has survived in continuous production until today. The factory was founded in 1751 by John Wall, a doctor of medicine, and William Davis, an apothecary. Experiments in Davis' chemist's shop were encouraging enough to attract thirteen other businessmen to invest their money, and a factory was built on the banks of the river Severn. Archaeology on the original site has shown initial attempts at making porcelain plates and dishes ended in failure and so, to save their investment, the partners bought the Bristol Porcelain factory from Miller and Lund. This gave them access to soaprock, and with new kilns the result during 1752 was the perfection of porcelain making at

The flower painting on this Worcester coffee cup and saucer was added in James Giles' London decorating establishment, c.1770. Giles copied the latest Meissen porcelain and Worcester have used fake Meissen marks here too.

Worcester. Worcester looked towards the London market and needed a product that would sell alongside the competition of the time. Chinese porcelain was now cheaper and Bow made inexpensive copies also. Chelsea mastered the Continental style and both of these London factories reproduced old Japan. Worcester were determined to be different, and they expanded on the unique products of Limehouse and Bristol – English silver shapes with mock-Chinese decoration.

The British public loved sauceboats and Worcester made these in great numbers. Vases proved popular and big jugs for beer or cider. Massive tureens were made, but Worcester had problems making large objects with their soaprock formula, for it tended to distort in the kiln. Unlike their rivals at Derby, Bow and

Chelsea, however, Worcester's porcelain could withstand hot liquids without cracking. Worcester therefore specialised in teasets, making wonderful teapots, and there was no need to compete with the other figure makers. Worcester made no figures at all until the late 1760s, and even then only a handful of different models. Instead, by 1757 Worcester were producing superb teawares in blue and white. Early moulded shapes had given way to very plain forms and patterns which were closer to Chinese. Fine potting and even glazing meant Worcester was now almost better than the Chinese imports, and they captured the lion's share of the English teaware market. During the 1750s Worcester was unmarked except for tiny workmen's symbols which are not fully understood. Around 1760 a factory mark of a neat painted crescent was introduced, no doubt as famous at the time as Chelsea's gold anchor. Other marks included copies of Meissen and a mock Chinese seal mark, but curiously, most coloured Worcester remained unmarked.

The defection of Robert Podmore to Liverpool lost Worcester their monopoly of making soaprock porcelain. Chaffers' factory competed with Worcester blue and white, but Worcester more than held their own thanks to the invention of transfer printing. Printing meant Worcester teasets were less expensive and every piece matched perfectly. Fine engravings, the best by Robert Hancock, were printed in black overglaze in perfect detail and commemorative mugs with portraits of the famous were sold in vast numbers. Richard Holdship sold the secret of Worcester's printing to Duesbury at Derby, but no other English factory approached the quality of Worcester's printing at this time.

During the 1760s the influence of Meissen was of increasing importance. Subsequently the introduction of coloured grounds, especially a deep blue and the celebrated 'scale blue', brought new fame to Worcester as the fashion for Sèvres developed. Chelsea had great difficulty controlling their mazarine blue, but Worcester overcame the problems and their blue-ground tablewares, with reserved rococo panels of birds or flowers, sold in large numbers and for high prices. European styles now dominated Worcester's production. At the same time copies of Oriental patterns were made for customers who wanted to replace broken pieces of family sets. Full services with popular Chinese figure patterns were also sold, but there was now no need to pretend these were anything other than Worcester porcelain, for its reputation had spread around the world. It was exported, especially to Holland, and copies of Worcester were now made by the Chinese themselves.

Some Worcester porcelain was painted in London in the studio of James Giles. The precise arrangement worked out between Giles and the Worcester factory remains unclear, but from the early 1760s white porcelain was sent from Worcester for decoration in London. Between 1767 and 1771, under a formal agree-

A Worcester 'Bishop Sumner' pattern plate, c.1775, a dramatic adaptation of a Chinese famille verte *design of fifty years before.*   Dyson Perrins Museum

ment, Giles' workshop was provided with all the white ware it needed and this was painted in the latest Continental styles exactly copying Meissen and Sèvres with a freshness not seen on Worcester factory-decorated porcelain.

Severe economic recession in the 1770s saw Worcester battle to survive, especially following the defection of Thomas Turner whose rival Caughley factory copied Worcester's popular blue-printed tablewares. Worcester struggled on into the 1780s as a moribund establishment making old-fashioned wares. The factory survived thanks to the London china dealer Thomas Flight who bought the business in 1783 for his sons. Young John Flight personally managed the company through very difficult times following a further defection in 1789 of the Chamberlain family who had supervised all of the decoration at Worcester and now set up their own rival business in Worcester. Flight opened a new London shop stocked mostly with French porcelain, and directed the factory to abandon their unprofitable blue and white in favour of the latest French styles and best gilding. John Flight turned the fortunes of the factory around, but tragically he died in 1791 aged only twenty-five. His brother Joseph was joined at Worcester

A Flight, Barr and Barr Worcester plate truly fit for a king, designed for the coronation of William IV in 1830. The quality is almost beyond belief. 10in. (25.5cm).

the following year by Martin Barr and the company traded as Flight and Barr. The factory mark was a tiny letter B scratched into the base.

Flights now followed Derby's lead and concentrated only on the best for the top end of the market. Every piece was finished with the finest gilding and gradually the wealthy customers returned to support the original Worcester factory. Orders from the King and the Duke of Clarence encouraged other nobility to request

services decorated with their family crests and Worcester armorial porcelain replaced Chinese sets in all of the greatest households. Changes in management led to name changes as the firm became Barr, Flight and Barr in 1804 and Flight, Barr and Barr in 1813, these names proudly written under every piece. During the Regency period superb painted decoration and lavish gilding resulted in some of the richest of all English porcelain, and the quality of their

'Japan' patterns outshone all other makers. Flights understood classical elegance but failed to notice that public taste wanted new French styles and rococo again in the 1820s and '30s. Left behind by fashion, the firm struggled once more and in 1840 they were forced to merge with their bitter rivals to become Chamberlain & Co.

Further reading
Lawrence Branyan, Neal French and John Sandon, *Worcester Blue and White Porcelain,* revised 1989
Henry Sandon, *Worcester Porcelain,* 1969
Henry Sandon, *Flight and Barr Worcester Porcelain*, ACC, 1992
John Sandon, *The Dictionary of Worcester Porcelain 1751-1851,* ACC, 1993
Simon Spero and John Sandon, *Worcester Porcelain, the Zorensky Collection,* ACC, 1997

A shell-shaped sweetmeat dish identified by the typically naïve painting as from the first years of the Lowestoft factory, 5½in. (14cm). c.1759-60.

---

10. LOWESTOFT

This Suffolk port seems an unlikely location for a major porcelain factory, yet, although it was never large, the Lowestoft china works survived successfully for more than forty years. A group of local businessmen headed by Philip Walker began to make blue and white around 1757. The phosphatic body, containing bone ash, resembles that of Bow, with a soft chalky appearance. Because of the highly absorbent unglazed body, blue patterns had to be painted quickly, resulting in the lively spontaneity that epitomises early Lowestoft. There is a delightful cartoon-like quality quite unlike the blue and white of Worcester.

No coloured decoration was attempted until the late 1760s, by which time the factory was supplying two very different markets. Blue and white mostly copied established designs from Worcester, and the Worcester mark of a crescent was blatantly copied along with shapes and patterns. This can be confusing, but it really is not difficult to distinguish the poor quality blue printing and heavy potting used at Lowestoft. Lowestoft enjoyed a keen trade with Holland, but in addition local customers were far more important in a provincial location than in London. The result was a large output of inscribed and dated pieces made for local families. These dated rarities have a great deal of charm, as do the exceedingly rare Lowestoft figures which naturally command high prices, but all Lowestoft porcelain seems expensive compared with other factories due to competition from keen East Anglian collectors who appreciate its naïve beauty. Meissen marks were copied as well as Worcester's crescent, but Lowestoft did not use a mark of its own. Instead many pieces of blue and white bear a painter's numeral on the base by the footrim.

The factory survived until 1799, when most other makers of soft paste porcelain were long forgotten. It is curious to think of Lowestoft as a contemporary of New Hall, but the coloured wares made during its final fifteen years copied the same cheap Chinese exports as the Staffordshire makers. Geoffrey Godden, a great enthusiast, has written of the 'homely charm' of the unpretentious Lowestoft porcelain, sentiments few can fail to echo.

Further reading
Geoffrey Godden, *Lowestoft Porcelains,* revised, ACC, 1985
Sheenah Smith, *Lowestoft Porcelain in Norwich Castle Museum,* two volumes, 1975 and 1985

A selection of blue and white Chaffers porcelain, c.1756-62. Although individual, the factory clearly took inspiration from Chinese and Worcester porcelain.

11. THE LIVERPOOL FACTORIES

As the Liverpool delftware industry declined, many potters turned their attention to porcelain. Owners and managers moved from one pot-works to another and workmen moved likewise, resulting in the confusion facing Liverpool collectors today. The most important factory was the Chaffers/Christian/Seth Pennington works on Shaw's Brow, but there were several other factories including at least two managed by other members of the Pennington family. Their productions were remarkably similar and research has only started to unravel the situation.

Samuel Gilbody took over his father's pottery on Shaw's Brow around 1754 and advertised porcelain for sale in 1758. Two years later he was bankrupt and nothing was known of his production until fragments of his kiln failures were discovered by Alan Smith close to where Liverpool Museum now stands. Gilbody's bone ash porcelain has a curious silky glaze, with runny underglaze blue and a distinctive palette of colours. Several figures were made and these are well modelled but most suffered severe firing problems. The factory's early demise means that Gilbody porcelain is rare and expensive today.

Richard Chaffers probably commenced porcelain manufacture in 1754 in partnership with Philip Christian. The earliest Chaffers 'phosphatic' porcelain containing bone ash was moderately successful with a noticeable grey cast to the paste and glaze. Robert Podmore defected from Worcester and agreed to provide Chaffers and Christian with soaprock. The resulting 'steatitic' porcelain was very similar to that of Worcester and probably went on sale for the first time at the end of 1756 when Chaffers guaranteed his porcelain against cracking with boiling water. Chaffers produced mostly blue and white in Chinese style, with some coloured wares, and like Worcester specialised in useful wares rather than ornamental. Chaffers died in

A mug from John Pennington's factory at Folly Lane in Liverpool, 1785-90. The handle shape is characteristic.   Bernard Watney collection

Samuel Gilbody's factory was plagued by firing problems and this vase is a rare survivor. The blue painting shows affinities with other Liverpool makers. 6in. (15cm), c.1758.

December 1765 and the factory was continued without any interruption by Philip Christian. There were no immediate changes, but during the Christian period the underglaze blue became paler, a greater use was made of enamel colours and there was more direct copying of Worcester. Fine moulded teapots and splendid coffee pots were made. Philip Christian and his son ran the factory until 1778 when it was taken over by Seth Pennington and John Part. They, or their successors, continued until 1803. Once again there was no sudden change in the factory's productions in 1778, and any attribution to Chaffers, Christian or Seth Pennington is entirely dependent on the likely date of manufacture. The quality of the underglaze blue declined significantly under Pennington and Part, but this was due to the economics of the time.

James Pennington had been a partner with Chaffers and Christian in 1755, and it is believed he set up as a porcelain maker on his own in 1763, working for about ten years. Elsewhere in Liverpool John Pennington began his own porcelain factory in 1770 and on his death in 1786 this was continued by his widow Jane Pennington until 1794. Archaeology has helped to unravel which Pennington made what, but a lot of research is still needed. In particular we do not know what porcelain was made in Liverpool by William Reid and William Ball who were operating from the mid-1750s until the late 1760s. Various theories have been put forward, but in the absence of any marked specimens it must be hoped archaeology can once more come to the rescue.

Further reading

Bernard Watney, *English Blue and White Porcelain*, revised 1973

Bernard Watney, *Liverpool Porcelain of the Eighteenth Century*, Richard Dennis Publications, 1997

Seriously distorted in the kiln, this sauceboat would not have been a credit to any maker, but in a sense it is very typical of Longton Hall. 7¼in. (18.5cm) long, c.1754.

12. LONGTON HALL AND WEST PANS

This is very much the personal achievement of William Littler, a Staffordshire potter whose name is associated with blue-glazed stoneware produced in partnership with his brother-in-law Aaron Wedgwood from 1745. Deep blue remained significant as a ground colour at Longton and later at West Pans. Littler entered into a new partnership with William Jenkinson who had commenced porcelain manufacture at Longton Hall prior to 1750. Early products were the so-called 'Snowman' type figures, well named from the appearance of the thick, semi-opaque glaze. The factory soon established its own unique style of rustic mayhem. Longton Hall is synonymous with leaves — by themselves, overlapping or embossed with trailing tendrils around the rims of plates and tureens, the centres enamelled with flowers in a distinctive style known as 'Trembly Rose'. The lurid green and yellow used on Longton's leaf shapes is unmistakable, and the eccentric forms themselves served to disguise the distortion of the glass-like 'frit' paste. Blue and white is of variable quality to say the least — frequently misshapen, or blurred, or both. At its best it barely equalled its competitors. The same was true of Longton Hall figures. Inferior to Chelsea, certainly, but not without considerable charm of their own, the charm of Staffordshire pottery.

Littler's factory survived ten difficult years, but while Worcester and other makers thrived, the Longton Hall venture was a failure, closing in 1760. Always out on its own as the sole porcelain maker in Staffordshire, even its bankruptcy sale of 90,000 pieces was held not in London but in Salisbury. Disillusioned, William Littler took his family to the wilderness of Scotland, setting up a china works near Musselburgh at West Pans. Here Littler used the same moulds and a similar body and glaze, and so it is hardly surprising the production at West Pans has been confused with earlier Longton Hall. Raised white enamel ornament and unfired oil gilding were used on the thick 'Littler's Blue' glaze, and armorials were painted alongside clumsy flowers for local Scottish families. A factory mark of a crossed letter L was occasionally used at West Pans. Money finally ran out in 1777 and Littler was forced to return once more to Staffordshire, joining Ralph Baddeley as manager at a porcelain works in Shelton.

Further reading

Geoffrey Godden (Ed.), *Staffordshire Porcelain*, 1983

Bernard Watney, *Longton Hall Porcelain*, 1957

Left, a Plymouth blue and white mustard pot in the distinctive, almost-black colour, 3in. (8cm), 'tin' mark. Right, a Bristol creamboat enamelled in puce, 6½in. (16.5cm) long, cross mark, c.1768-72.

13. PLYMOUTH AND BRISTOL

The first true or hard paste porcelain to be fired successfully in England was the result of years of experiment by William Cookworthy, an apothecary who discovered the vital combination of kaolin and china stone in Cornwall. Plymouth's porcelain was similar to Meissen and investors in Cookworthy's factory must have had high expectations as the first wares were put on sale in 1768. Today surviving pieces tell part of a sad story, however, displaying the results of disastrous glaze firings which ruined so much of the porcelain. A smoky grey glaze often spattered with soot, dirty opaque enamels and severe distortion of the body show the difficulties Cookworthy experienced, forcing the closure of the factory in 1770.

The Plymouth factory had advertised for painters in Worcester newspapers so it is hardly surprising blue and white Plymouth occurs with popular Worcester patterns. The factory mark used at Plymouth, resembling the combined numerals 2 and 4, was the alchemists' sign for tin.

It is uncertain what precisely was made at the Bristol factory between 1770 and 1774 and it is possible much that is at present attributed to Cookworthy at Plymouth was actually made by him a few years later at Bristol. Figures on

rococo bases, and shell salts are remarkably similar to Bow, due to the modeller John Toulouse who started his career at Bow and who also worked at Worcester. His mark of a letter T occurs on all these porcelains. In due course new kilns at Bristol corrected the problem of the smoky glaze, thanks to Richard Champion, a Bristol merchant who took over Cookworthy's patent for making true porcelain when the latter retired in 1774. Bristol porcelain is usually a beautiful white colour, but it was still dogged by firing difficulties, causing tears in the paste and the distinctive spiral 'wreathing' as vessels twisted, in the direction they had been formed, in the intense heat of the kiln. To prevent bases sagging, concentric rings or lines of clay were built up to reinforce the undersides of plates and dishes.

Bristol based most of its decorative styles on Meissen, copying the latest patterns. Meissen had not been on sale in England since the Seven Years War and Bristol copies of the crossed swords and dot mark, used at Meissen from 1763-1774, must have been added to pass off the Bristol wares as genuine German porcelain. Other marks used at Bristol were a cross, and the letter B, often accompanied by workmen's numerals.

Neo-classical taste had replaced rococo and, as at Chelsea-Derby, Bristol particularly

An early New Hall sugar box and a tea canister, well potted and elegant with formal border patterns inspired by France rather than China, the canister 4½in. (11.5cm), c.1785.

favoured the use of green monochrome. Champion's figures are a considerable improvement on Cookworthy's, but still are far inferior to Derby. One area where Bristol did excel, however, was in biscuit flower modelling seen on a series of portrait plaques. Although some fine porcelain was made at Bristol, it was expensive to produce and overall it was a commercial failure. Champion closed the factory in 1781, having attempted to sell his true porcelain patent to Staffordshire potters.

Further reading
F. Severne MacKenna, *Cookworthy's Plymouth and Bristol Porcelain,* 1946; and *Champion's Bristol Porcelain,* 1947

14. NEW HALL

Richard Champion, facing severe financial losses, arrived in Staffordshire in 1780 or '81 in an attempt to sell what remained of his patent for making true porcelain. Josiah Wedgwood

felt sorry for him and, while not interested himself, he did suggest a list of potters who might be prepared to invest in a new Staffordshire porcelain factory. Ten prominent pottery manufacturers were impressed by Champion's new experiments and put up the money to construct a factory at the New Hall in Shelton. The recipe had developed from the Bristol china body and was now a new type of porcelain that has become known as 'hybrid hard paste'. The company owned by the pottery-making shareholders went by various partnership names, principally Heath, Warburton & Co. and then Hollins, Warburton & Co, while the firm was managed for them by John Daniel. Their product was known as Shelton China or the China from New Hall.

New Hall porcelain lacked the whiteness of Bristol, but it was durable, free of potting problems and undoubtedly was highly successful. The owners were interested only in profit and avoided expensive ornamental ware. The concentration was on teawares supplied to

The 'Window' pattern, one of New Hall's most popular designs painted over a transfer-printed outline, 9¾in. (25cm), c.1800-10.

china shops, with repeated border patterns. These copied contemporary Chinese, elegant French and smart Georgian patterns to suit every taste. To assist the china dealers, New Hall pioneered the use of pattern numbers which are of vital benefit to collectors today. Underglaze blue prints were well controlled, as was overglaze bat printing which was usually hand-coloured. Free-hand painting was against the factory's general principals, but Fidelle Duvivier was engaged as a decorator for a small number of teasets and mugs in his distinctive Continental style. The hybrid hard paste body had been very successful, but eventually could not compete with the whiter bone china. New Hall switched to making the new china around 1814. Early New Hall porcelain is famous today, and it is easy to forget that the company continued into the 1830s, by which time it had become just another Staffordshire factory, competent but not exceptional.

Apart from pattern numbers and occasional workmen's symbols, factory marks were not used until the bone china body when a name mark of 'New Hall' within concentric circles was printed on some pieces. Without marks and pattern numbers, collectors identify New Hall by shape. Most shapes are unique and it is important to learn them, for New Hall had many imitators. The partners had reached a special agreement to use Champion's recipes but they did not hold any patent. Some partners made porcelain on their own account, while many other makers produced a very similar hybrid hard paste body. Shapes and patterns were copied too. Some makers, such as Coalport, have been positively identified. Many others remain stubbornly anonymous, even though their convenience names of Factory X and Factory Z have become almost legendary.

Further reading

Geoffrey Godden, *Encyclopaedia of British Porcelain Manufacturers,* 1988

David Holgate, *New Hall and Its Imitators,* 1971 and the revised version, *New Hall,* 1987

Although copying a cheap Chinese export teaware pattern, this Caughley coffee pot is finely potted and graceful too, 8½in. (21.5cm), c.1785.

15. CAUGHLEY

Coalport's outrageous claim to have been founded in 1750 stems from the possible date Ambrose Gallimore set up a pottery works at Caughley, a small village in Shropshire. Extensive archaeology on the Caughley site has yielded precious little evidence of Gallimore's pottery, but plenty of clues to the productions of the Caughley China Works established when Thomas Turner joined Gallimore in 1772. While at Worcester, Turner had been much more than an engraver training under Robert Hancock. He is believed to have been responsible for retail sales and understood clearly which area of Worcester's production was the most profitable – the inexpensive but popular blue prints.

The Caughley porcelain body was identical to Worcester's soaprock formula, although the glaze tends to be slightly creamier. The theory that Turner took with him to Caughley many of the best craftsmen from Worcester cannot be proven, but from the outset Caughley made established Worcester shapes and patterns and, if anything, these are better potted, and printed with greater care than the Worcester prototypes. Turner saw no need to make costly enamelled and gilded porcelain. Instead he targeted the middle market, supplying teasets, dinner services and other useful tableware shapes copying the best-selling porcelain in the china shops of the time – Chinese 'Nankin', French imports with simple sprig patterns, and of course Worcester printed wares. Worcester had supplied an important export market in blue and white china to Holland and Caughley produced the same baskets, butter tubs, salad dishes and mask jugs (known as 'Dutch Jugs'). The delightful Caughley miniatures or 'Toys' must have found a ready market in Holland also.

Caughley did make a small quantity of enamelled porcelain, mostly cheap and clumsy. Between about 1788 and 1793 Caughley white porcelain was sold to the Chamberlain family in Worcester where it was decorated and richly gilded in competition with Flight's factory. This arrangement came to an end when the Chamberlains began to make their own porcelain. Caughley marked its blue and white with less frequency than Worcester, using a letter C as opposed to Worcester's crescent. Salopian, the old name for Shropshire, was impressed on some flatware, while the initial letter S was more widely used. Distinguishing unmarked Caughley from Worcester can be difficult, but there are generally differences in the printed patterns and the shape of the footrim varies, Caughley favouring a long square footrim section as opposed to Worcester's triangular profile. Some time in the mid-1790s Caughley gave up the soaprock formula in favour of a hybrid hard paste of the type developed at New Hall. This was not a success, although it continued to be made at the Caughley works into the nineteenth century under the direction of John Rose & Co. of Coalport, for Thomas Turner sold out to his rival in 1799.

Further reading

Geoffrey Godden, *Caughley and Worcester Porcelain,* revised, ACC, 1981

A group of Pinxton jardinières with separate bases, 4in. (10.5cm) and 5¾in. (14.5cm), c.1798. William Billingsley realised French porcelain was the fashion in London and copied Parisian shapes and designs.

16. PINXTON

While it was John Coke who financed a porcelain factory on his estate at Pinxton in Derbyshire, William Billingsley provided the necessary expertise to produce beautiful soft-paste porcelain. During twenty years at Derby, Billingsley became England's foremost flower painter, but he also learnt every aspect of porcelain manufacture. Derby was sad to lose him, and horrified to discover that he was to begin making an almost identical porcelain just fifteen miles away. The first Pinxton china went on sale in 1797, copying popular shapes made at Derby and Worcester, with patterns in the latest French manner. Some pieces were painted by Billingsley himself with his characteristic flowers or landscapes. These are seen at their best on bough pots – semicircular ornaments for bulbs on a mantelpiece, or on stunning cabaret sets. Tea services were

decorated with simple border patterns that are elegant and never dull. The painted name mark of Pinxton was occasionally used, while pattern numbers were often prefixed with a letter P, aiding identification.

The study of Pinxton porcelain is complex and has been much confused. Billingsley remained at Pinxton for only two and a half years; his partnership with Coke dissolved in April 1799. Billingsley moved to Mansfield and then Torksey where he worked as a decorator and subsequently made further porcelain. John Coke continued the Pinxton works, by himself and in partnership with Henry Banks. Later the site was leased to John Cutts, a china painter from Derby. Some porcelain was made at Pinxton after Billingsley's departure, probably up until the closure of the factory in 1813, but during this time decoration was mostly added to old stock, left in the white because of unsatisfactory firing. Several groups

139

A single dish from a sandwich or supper set, c.1810. This chinoiserie pattern, curiously inspired by early Meissen, proved popular at the Davenport factory.

of porcelain, formerly attributed to Pinxton and dating from around 1800, have since been reattributed. Enamelled marks of a letter A, a crescent and star, a sunburst and a Chinese precious symbol, occur on tablewares painted with border patterns in similar taste to Pinxton. The porcelain has been shown to be of Derby origin, however, with patterns added by independent decorators using inferior Derby wares sold in the white as faulty stock.

Further reading

Nicholas Gent, *The Shapes and Patterns of the Pinxton China Factory,* 1996
C. Barry Sheppard, *Pinxton Porcelain*, 1996

---

17. DAVENPORT

John Davenport, a former china dealer from Dublin, began making earthenware at Longport in Staffordshire probably in 1795. During his long career Davenport made many different types of pottery and stoneware, but it is his porcelain which concerns us here. Many factories adopted a hybrid hard paste formula around 1800 and Davenport's early china body is similar to many others, consequently identification is difficult as few pieces are marked. The painted marks 'Longport', or an

impressed anchor with the name Davenport, occur on some ornamental vases and bough pots, as well as rare table services. The shapes used were individual, with pleasing baskets to accompany dessert sets, and most unusual bifurcated handles on some teawares. One distinctive painting style from the early period features bold, ripe fruit. This occurs on early bone china sets, for the factory switched from the hybrid paste around 1808-10.

Davenport remained primarily a potter. Porcelain was never made in any great quantity and this generally mirrored the popular fashions of the time. Classical designs were favoured above the overtly rococo forms preferred by Coalport and Rockingham. Particularly splendid vases in the style of the French Empire were made in the 1820s, and from this time a high proportion of Davenport porcelain is marked, in red or underglaze blue. A magnificent service was made for the coronation of William IV and other suites for royal banquets led to the proud claim 'Manufacturers to their Majesties' added to some marks. One speciality of the factory in the midnineteenth century was the manufacture of porcelain plaques, the thinnest and best seen in England, with the mark 'Davenport Patent' stamped into the edge. It must be remembered that these were sold to independent china

A fruit dish from a Ridgway dessert service, c.1828-30, with typical formal flower painting, 9¾in. (25cm).

painters and the artists who occasionally signed their plaques did not work at the Davenport factory. Davenport made some impressive dessert sets in the third quarter of the nineteenth century, but avoided ornamental shapes such as vases and figures and was one of the few major porcelain makers not to attempt parian. The factory generally struggled in its later years and during the 1880s was reduced to making copies of Derby's popular Imari patterns. The works closed in 1887.

Further reading

Geoffrey Godden and Terence Lockett, *Davenport Earthenware, Porcelain and Glass*

---

18. RIDGWAY AND THE CAULDON PLACE WORKS

A complicated family history and several different Ridgway factories in Staffordshire have naturally left collectors confused, but, as far as porcelain making is concerned, there is a clear progression from one family business to another. The story starts when Job Ridgway opened an earthenware factory at Cauldon Place

in 1802. The first porcelain was made in 1808, the same year that he took his two sons into the business. Rare porcelain marked Ridgway & Sons dates from 1808-14. Job died in 1814 and John and William Ridgway continued in partnership until 1830, making fine porcelain as well as earthenware. A well-controlled body and neat glaze give a feeling of quality to all of the J. & W. Ridgway porcelain. Shapes suit the period without extravagance, and the decoration is usually tasteful. Deep blue or white grounds were favoured with flower or landscape painting, carefully finished with bright gilding. The two brothers went separate ways in 1830. William concentrated on earthenwares, while John continued the works at Cauldon Place in the same traditions of practical quality. Patterns from the 1835-45 period can be extremely complicated with flowers and gilding squeezed into every space, for this was the early Victorian taste. John Ridgway made some of the finest tea and dessert sets at this time, but few ornaments other than baskets, and no figures are recorded. The proud mark of the Royal Arms was used by John Ridgway, with the rare addition in about 1850 of 'By Royal Appointment Potter to Her Majesty'. Many unmarked Ridgway pieces can

An inkstand from a rich Spode desk set in one of their most costly designs, no. 1166 in the factory pattern book, 7¾in. (20cm) wide, c.1820-25.

be identified by pattern numbers, especially tea and dessert wares when fractional numbers with 2/ and 5/ prefixes were used.

Around 1855 John Ridgway took new partners into his business, trading as J. Ridgway, Bates and Co. In June 1858 John Ridgway retired and the firm continued as Bates, Brown-Westhead, & Co. Thomas Brown-Westhead and several partners continued the Cauldon Place works after 1861 as Brown-Westhead, Moore & Co. until 1904. This partnership continued to specialise in good quality dessert sets, but made a wide range of other ornamental china including good Parian figures and Limoges Enamel work by Thomas John Bott. Rarely marked, the later Cauldon Place porcelain can often be identified only by design registration marks. Possibly because the factory name is such a mouthful, the firm is not held in great regard by collectors, and good pieces by Brown-Westhead, Moore & Co. are definitely undervalued.

Further reading

Geoffrey Godden, *Ridgway Porcelain,* revised ACC, 1985

Geoffrey Godden (Ed.), *Staffordshire Porcelain,* 1983

19. SPODE AND COPELAND

Josiah Spode was one of many Staffordshire earthenware makers who turned their attention to porcelain at the end of the eighteenth century, but instead of making the hybrid hard paste body favoured elsewhere, Spode is generally credited with the invention of bone china, first produced around 1796-97. Although most early bone china was prone to staining, the early Spode body is usually surprisingly white, thin and free of crazing. In this respect it resembles French porcelain of the time, for the simple border patterns used at Spode have a very Continental feel. Blue printed patterns in Chinese style were widely used, and the factory produced high quality overglaze prints using bat printing techniques. Early pieces were marked with the Spode name impressed or painted along with the pattern number. Unmarked pieces can be recognised by their clean, well-modelled shapes.

Profits from earthenware subsidised porcelain manufacture, allowing Spode to concentrate on high quality decoration. Spode developed a distinctive style of its own, partly classical, partly oriental, making fine use of Japan patterns sparkling with brilliant gold. The

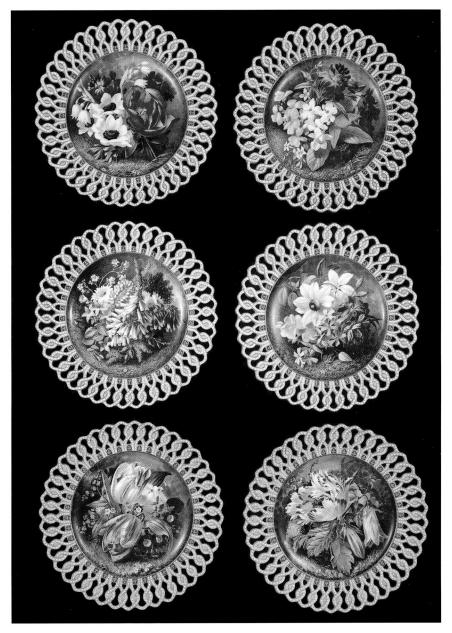

Copeland plates by the talented flower painter C.F. Hürten, 9¼in. (23.5cm), from a rich dessert service dated 1885. With such intricate jewelled borders, these were made for display only and not for use.

decoration at Spode prior to 1822 had been supervised by Henry Daniel who left in that year to set up his own china factory also in Stoke. Spode continued its elegant Regency style porcelain throughout the 1820s, falling behind its competitors in terms of fashion, but keeping an eye on quality, so that every piece of its 'Felspar Porcelain' was perfectly decorated.

Dramatic changes occurred after 1833 when the firm was taken over by William Copeland and Thomas Garrett who had managed their London retail operation. Some traditional Spode patterns continued, but Copeland and Garrett introduced up-to-date designs to compete with Coalport and other leading English makers supplying London china shops. Rococo revival and typically Victorian patterns were competently made, but the factory became just one of many, and collectors lament the changes that had replaced Spode's more unique style. Earthenware manufacture remained of greater importance than porcelain, but during the Copeland and Garrett period a major development came about with the introduction of 'Statuary Porcelain', better known as Parian. Garrett retired from the firm in 1847, leaving William Copeland in sole charge. Copeland spent much of his time in London, becoming an Alderman and Lord Mayor, but he successfully managed his factory and exploited the commercial potential of Parian alongside a massive earthenware production. Copeland reproduced in Parian the finest work of the leading sculptors of the day, models that sold in quite incredible numbers.

Alderman Copeland retired in 1867 and the works were continued by his four sons, but without their father's guidance the firm lost direction. When Parian fell from fashion, Copeland never really recovered. Fine flower painting by Charles F. Hürten and figure subjects by Samuel Alcock show the firm could produce fine work, but once the twentieth century arrived, Royal Worcester and other English makers left Copeland far behind. The factory continues to the present, having reverted to the original Spode name in 1970.

Further reading
Geoffrey Godden (Ed.), *Staffordshire Porcelain*, 1983
Leonard Whiter, *Spode*, revised 1978

20. COALPORT

Two rival factories sharing one site on the banks of the river Severn, managed by brothers both named Rose – no wonder the study of early Coalport porcelain is confusing! John and Thomas Rose probably both trained at the Caughley factory. John left to set up his own porcelain factory, first at Calcut near Jackfield in about 1794, moving to Coalport by 1796. Here he made blue-printed porcelain using a similar hybrid hard paste body to that introduced at Caughley at about the same time. A series of dated jugs have helped to identify the early John Rose porcelain, and vital information has come from factory site excavations. Thomas Turner, blaming ill health, sold his interests in Caughley to John Rose in 1799, but production continued at the Caughley works until 1814. Meanwhile Thomas Rose (trading first as Reynolds, Horton & Rose and then as Anstice, Horton and Rose) set up his own porcelain factory in 1800, right next door to his brother with only a canal separating their premises. Both firms made very similar shapes and identical patterns (but with different pattern numbers), ranging from simple New Hall-type designs to rich Japan patterns. Very careful study of the shapes is essential to identify any piece of early Coalport. Thomas Rose probably sold his factory to his brother in 1814 at the time of the closure of the Caughley works.

John Rose believed in mass production and made only a limited range of different shapes. Popular patterns were made in large quantities, as his factory became the biggest porcelain producer in the country. The quality of potting varies, and the decoration more so, as a large amount of Coalport was sold 'in the white' to independent decorators. Little is known about most of the amateur china painters who signed and dated their work on Coalport blanks, but some of the London studios, including Thomas

Typical Coalport products. Left, a 'Coalbrookdale' vase, c.1835. Centre, a plate by John Randall, c.1845. Right, a tureen in Sèvres style with flowers by William Cook, c.1850.

Baxter's workshop, produced exceptional decoration. Coalport probably switched from a hybrid body to bone china in 1815. The addition of a locally mined felspar produced a fine white body which won them a coveted Society of Arts Gold Medal in 1820. A large circular mark, announcing this award, was introduced in 1820 and continued to be used up to thirty years later. The date on the mark cannot be used to date the porcelain, therefore.

When his Welsh porcelain ventures failed, William Billingsley was employed by John Rose. It has been claimed that Coalport reused some of the Swansea moulds, but more likely they just continued to supply the same London customers with popular shapes, while decorators in London used Coalport blanks in place of previous supplies from Nantgarw. Coalport followed fashion in London very closely and introduced copies of the latest styles from Paris and Meissen in particular. Coalport porcelain encrusted with delicate

china flowers is traditionally thought of as a very English craft, but most shapes were exact copies of Meissen and many were marked with fake crossed swords as well as CD for Coalbrookdale, the name by which the rococo porcelain was known. Copies were made of old Chelsea and Sèvres and these were also sold with fake marks. Old Caughley printing plates, discovered lying about the factory, were re-used around 1850-60 to make copies of early Worcester, complete with crescent marks. Coalport generally marked its own name only on its richest productions. These include the work of two fine decorators, William Cook who painted flowers in Sèvres style, and John Randall, whose celebrated exotic birds are unmistakable. Unmarked Coalport tableware can be identified from the pattern numbers, usually neatly written in gold and following a successive series of fractional numbers, never exceeding 1000. Later in the nineteenth century copies of Worcester's Limoges enamel and

A toy cup and saucer or 'cabinet cup' decorated with fine jewels of turquoise enamel which were the speciality of the Coalport factory around 1900.

jewelled porcelain were attempted. The latter, using gold grounds set with tiny turquoise droplets, brought Coalport considerable acclaim, especially in the United States. From 1875 Coalport used a mark of a crown with the name Coalport and AD 1750, the preposterous date they claimed to have been established, which just happened to be one year before Worcester. After 1900 a series of impressed letters and numerals give the date of manufacture on many pieces, the last numbers denoting the year. Fine vases with painted panels and deep blue grounds were made in the early 1900s, but economic problems forced the closure of the factory in 1926. The work-force moved to Staffordshire where the factory continues, now owned by the Wedgwood group. The old Coalport factory, once derelict, is now preserved as an exciting museum.

Further reading

Geoffrey Godden, *Coalport and Coalbrook-dale Porcelain,* 1970, revised ACC, 1981
Michael Messenger, *Coalport,* ACC, 1996

21. WEDGWOOD

As Britain's foremost pottery manufacturer, Josiah Wedgwood stubbornly refused to become involved in the making of porcelain until his London showroom cried out for porcelain teawares to sell. The first Wedgwood bone china appeared in 1812 and, having waited so long, the firm had learnt from others' mistakes. They used the very best formula known at that time and produced an immaculate white, almost eggshell china with a tight glaze that rarely stains or crazes. Their purest pottery shapes were adapted for a small range of teawares, decorated with Chinese, Japanese and English patterns, mostly used previously on Wedgwood's earthenware. Delightful monochrome landscapes were painted by John Cutts who had come from Pinxton, and only the very best gold was used to emphasise the rims. As a mark Wedgwood used their name stencilled in red. Although incredibly elegant, bone china was not a commercial success at this time and production was gradually curtailed during the 1820s.

Three simple Wedgwood bone china coffee cans, c.1815. The patterns reflect the taste of English Regency with a mix of old Japan, 2½in. (6.2cm), red stencil marks.

Wedgwood subsequently returned to bone china in 1878, largely it would seem to make designs derivative from other manufacturers. Late Victorian Wedgwood bone china is very well made, thin and perfectly fired, but generally unimaginative. This changed in the twentieth century when Daisy Makeig-Jones designed the 'Fairyland' range along with other designs in lustreware. Curious, colourful, highly decorative, these pieces were costly in the 1920s but bought by connoisseurs for their enjoyment. Fairyland lustre is understandably expensive today too (see page 39). Wedgwood has remained foremost a pottery maker, but in recent years bone china dinner ware has played a vital role in the factory's international success.

Further reading
Maureen Batkin, *Wedgwood Ceramics 1846-1959*, 1982
Geoffrey Godden (Ed.), *Staffordshire Porcelain*, 1983

22. MILES MASON

As a prominent china dealer, Miles Mason became wealthy trading in Chinese Export porcelain, but the East India Company grew tired of London dealers fixing the prices and stopped importing Oriental china. His livelihood threatened, Mason looked to the production of English china to replace the Chinese blue and white dinner sets he used to sell so

readily. A short partnership with Thomas Wolfe in Liverpool produced blue-printed teawares, but this failed in 1800. Mason moved to Staffordshire and in 1802 established a major porcelain works at Lane Delph, making hybrid hard paste. In 1804 Mason was able to claim his porcelain was more beautiful and more durable than the Chinese Nankin china. It was certainly better potted, but to see how some Mason's pieces have cracked and stained over the years, his porcelain was clearly not as durable as he liked to think. English patterns

A 'Nankin' pattern, not painted in far-away China but transfer printed in Miles Mason's factory in Staffordshire, 9in. (23cm), impressed mark M.Mason, c.1805-10.

This plate shows two techniques at which the Minton factory excelled. The centre is pâte-sur-pâte by Alboin Birks, while the border is in top quality raised paste gilding, 9½in. (24cm), dated 1911.

Minton's cloisonné decoration copied the best Oriental metalwork on a luscious turquoise enamel ground. The pattern is purely Chinese, while the shape is old French Sèvres, 8¼in. (21cm), c.1872

were made alongside Chinese designs. A neat impressed mark 'M.MASON' was used, as well as mock Chinese seal marks in blue, but Mason was not alone in using such seal marks.

In 1813 Miles Mason passed the business on to his two sons, George and Charles James. It was Charles James who introduced the famous 'Patent Ironstone China' which was not china at all but a hard earthenware. Porcelain was discontinued at this time, but later in his career C.J. Mason experimented with bone china, making in china some of the same shapes and patterns used for the Ironstone. Other teawares made by Mason in his porcelain c.1840-45 are totally eccentric both in shape and pattern – of moderate quality but certainly individual.

Further reading

Geoffrey Godden, *Mason's China and the Ironstone Wares,* revised ACC, 1980

---

23. MINTON

Minton is the most exciting English porcelain factory, for the variety of its products is quite extraordinary. Thomas Minton started the firm,

making blue-printed earthenware in Stoke-on-Trent in 1796, having learnt engraving as an apprentice at Caughley. Porcelain was probably first produced in 1798, also printed in blue in the Chinese manner. Minton made bone china rather than a hybrid hard paste, and early wares were prone to crazing and staining. Few of the early Minton teawares are exceptional although some Japan patterns can be pleasantly bold. From about 1805 Minton used a mark based on part of the crossed Ls of Sèvres, with the letter M and a pattern number.

Production of china stopped about 1816 and did not resume until 1824, probably at the instigation of Herbert Minton. By this time the problem of crazing was a thing of the past. Unlike other Staffordshire makers, Minton was accomplished both in tea and dessert ware production and wonderful ornamental porcelain. During the 1830s vases and figures look to the Continent, copying the latest imports especially from Meissen. Minton epitomises the so-called 'English Dresden'. Classical or rococo, the same shapes were made plain or covered in finely modelled flowers. Landscape and floral painting has a delicate subtlety not found in Worcester or Derby. Figures copy Meissen exactly but retain

A complete Minton desk set in the French taste that proved popular in England in the 1830s. Minton gilding at this time was simply superb. The tray 16¾in. (42.5cm) wide.

the charm of Staffordshire too.

Thomas Minton died in 1836 and his son Herbert continued what had become a very large family business. Herbert loved porcelain and under his direction the factory concentrated further on quality. The greatest porcelain of the past — magnificent eighteenth century Sèvres — was borrowed and carefully copied as an exercise in craftsmanship as much as a commercial venture. Léon Arnoux came from Sèvres as Art Director along with many other French artists, breathing fresh life into English porcelain. Mock Sèvres vases were displayed alongside Parian at the Great Exhibition, glorifying the past and the present, and showing that Minton could look ahead as well as back.

Herbert died in 1858 but the firm continued to bear his name as Herbert Minton & Co. The 1870s and '80s saw their greatest achievements. Minton discovered Japan and produced an incredible range of curious designs borrowed from the exciting wares of the East. Their cloisonné range reproduced the brilliant colours of Oriental metalwork on fantastic new shapes, some designed by Dr Christopher Dresser. Above all else, Minton is famed for its pâte-sur-pâte, whereby a design was built up in white clay on a darker ground before glazing. The greatest exponent was Marc Louis Solon

whose fantasy world of Cupids and maidens borders on the perverse. His many pupils included Alboin Birks who also produced wonderful pâte-sur-pâte, and their work was always finished off with exquisite gilding.

Yet the towering achievements of Victorian Minton somehow turned sour overnight. The firm relied too heavily on mass-produced cheap earthenware using old fashioned designs. Attempts were made to modernise production with a brilliant young Art Director John Wadsworth, but his Art Nouveau and Secessionist designs inspired by Paris and Vienna were only produced half-heartedly, especially in porcelain. The decline was rapid and although fine and practical dinner services continued to be made, twentieth century Minton presents a sad reminder of past glory. From 1860 onwards most Minton is clearly marked with the factory name and usually a date code too, a different symbol for each year stamped into the clay.

Further reading

Paul Atterbury and Maureen Batkin, *Dictionary of Minton*, ACC, 1990

Geoffrey Godden, *Minton Pottery and Porcelain,* 1968

Joan Jones, *Minton: The First Two Hundred Years of Design and Production*, 1993.

A covered chocolate cup from Lord Nelson's breakfast set. When Nelson visited Chamberlain's factory in 1802 he ordered a set in the 'Japan' style much in vogue at that time. Marked with pattern no. 240.

24. CHAMBERLAIN

Robert Chamberlain had been a key figure at Flight's Worcester factory where he supervised the entire decorating department. His employers were devastated when he left in 1786, for Chamberlain took many of the painters and gilders with him and, to make matters worse, they took over Flight's old shop in Worcester High Street and ran it under the Chamberlain name. Initially they sold only Caughley porcelain with enamelling and gilding added in their own workshop. Thomas Turner was interested only in blue and white and was happy to provide Chamberlain with white porcelain blanks. By 1791 Chamberlain were making their own porcelain, of a hybrid hard paste type. Early Chamberlain teasets were decorated in the same fashion as rivals Flight and Barr, with blue and gold borders in the French style. John Wood painted classical figure subjects, and views of Worcester, Cheltenham and other popular resorts were

painted often in monochrome. Early firing problems, causing a speckled smoky glaze, were slowly resolved and by 1802, when Lord Nelson visited Worcester, the factory was thriving. Their speciality was armorial porcelain, as well as rich Japan patterns featuring very bright gilding. Nelson's order for a breakfast service reflected both of these fashions. Chamberlain made fine ornamental porcelain although vases were rarely large. Instead they found a ready market for desk sets, spill vases and souvenir card trays painted with pretty scenes, flowers, birds or just feathers. Many delightful small animal models were made as well as amusing figures. Chamberlain enjoyed the patronage of the Prince of Wales and named their superior porcelain body 'Regent China' in his honour. Heavy competition, from Staffordshire as well as the two other Worcester factories, caused hardship and in 1840 Chamberlain and Flight, Barr and Barr amalgamated to become Chamberlain & Co., continuing production at

A pair of Grainger, Lee and Co. vases representing the more delicate side of the rococo revival of the 1830s. These are in biscuit porcelain with beautiful hand-made flowers, 12¼in. (31cm).

Chamberlain's factory in Diglis, the site of the present Worcester porcelain works. Some fine decoration continued into the 1840s, but general production was inferior to the principal Staffordshire makers. Walter Chamberlain, the last of his family to be involved in the business, retired in 1851 and the works were subsequently continued by Kerr and Binns, becoming the Worcester Royal Porcelain Co. in 1862.

Further reading

Geoffrey Godden, *Chamberlain-Worcester Porcelain,* 1982

John Sandon, *Dictionary of Worcester Porcelain,* ACC, 1993

25. GRAINGER

Always thought of as the third Worcester factory, the firm of Grainger & Co. survived for nearly a hundred years, far longer than many of its rivals in Staffordshire. It is more appropriate to compare Grainger with Staffordshire, for its productions were very different from the other Worcester makers. Grainger specialised in teasets and dinner wares, often with inexpensive printed patterns. Ornamental porcelain was certainly made, and the best Grainger vases match the productions of Chamberlain. Thomas Grainger had been an apprentice at Chamberlain's and set up on his own in a partnership trading as Grainger, Wood

The King and Queen as seen by an unknown Staffordshire porcelain maker at the time of their coronation in 1830, the bases proudly titled in gold. Great fun.

& Co. Their first porcelain, made in 1806, was similar to the other Worcester makers — spiral fluted teasets with gilded borders, and bright Japan patterns. In 1811 the firm became Thomas Grainger & Co., and from 1817-1837 the name of Grainger, Lee & Co. was used. Their finest porcelain dates from this period, especially a series of biscuit vases applied with modelled flowers or vines, and little trays and baskets painted with views of Worcester. George Grainger managed the factory following his father Thomas' death in 1839, but little original or memorable was made until the 1870s when a Parian body was used for a range of finely pierced or 'reticulated' vases and cabinet wares. In 1889 Frank Grainger sold the family business to the rival Worcester Royal Porcelain Co. who continued to run the works as a separate operation until 1902, using the name 'Royal China Works'. Shaded ivory

grounds were the speciality of the later Grainger factory. Several great twentieth century artists began their careers at Grainger's including James and John Stinton.

Further reading
Henry and John Sandon, *Grainger's Worcester Porcelain,* 1989
John Sandon, *Dictionary of Worcester Porcelain,* ACC, 1993

26. STAFFORDSHIRE PORCELAIN ORNAMENTS

In his comprehensive reference book, *Encyclopaedia of British Porcelain Manufacturers,* Geoffrey Godden lists the names of many Staffordshire makers whose productions are unknown. Most made tea and dinner sets for everyday use, sold through china shops who

Samuel Alcock's factory in Burslem was responsible for these most splendid porcelain leopards, c.1840, 7in. (18cm) wide, impressed model no. 255.

did not like manufacturers marking their wares. Many of these little factories also made vases and other ornaments, as well as figures and animal models, in earthenware and bone china. Rare marked examples give us the names of a few factories, but most carry no identification. Their makers would probably have been quite proud for their wares to be known simply as 'Staffordshire', for here was the heart of their industry.

Samuel Alcock & Co., who operated the Hill Pottery in Burslem, can be identified as the maker of many charming animal models from the discovery of broken fragments unearthed in Staffordshire bearing a distinctive form of model number stamped into the bases. Sheep and poodles have woolly coats made from clay pushed through a sieve, and modelled rockwork bases are carefully shaded and edged with a gold line. Many other makers produced similar sheep models and there is a long tradition for such pieces to be attributed to Rockingham, but while the Rockingham factory did make some little animals, most are clearly marked and only a small number of subjects were made. Thankfully most are now called Staffordshire again, but they are destined to remain anonymous, as are the charming models or rustic cottages

which form pastille burners. Poor sanitation meant that a Staffordshire cottage was vital in every room in a town house in London, the sweet-smelling smoke drifting from the chimneys to disguise the stink of the drains outside (see page 31). Delightful collections of Staffordshire animals and cottages can be formed and most are not expensive today.

John and Rebecca Lloyd ran a porcelain factory in Shelton in Staffordshire between 1834 and 1852, specialising in charming but inexpensive porcelain figures and animal models. Marked examples have helped identify some of their poodles and spaniels, as well as figures including Queen Victoria and Albert. The Lloyd's Staffordshire figures are certainly not great works of art, but they are well made of their type and absolutely full of charm (see page 113). There is a tendency to attribute many porcelain figures to Lloyd of Shelton, but again it is important to remember that many other makers produced similar goods during the 1840s.

Further Reading

Anthony Oliver, *Staffordshire Pottery, The Tribal Art of England*, 1981

Clive Mason-Pope, *A-Z of Staffordshire Dogs*, ACC, 1996

This specimen plate was one of several provided for William IV to choose the design for his Rockingham dinner service ordered in 1830. This rejected design featured a semi-burnished pattern on the gold panels, 9½in. (24cm), griffin mark.

27. ROCKINGHAM

Misunderstood, and much maligned for its eccentric productions, Rockingham deserves proper study to appreciate the contribution this provincial factory made to the British porcelain industry. Rockingham is indeed individual, and much does seem in questionable taste today, but at the time it was made this porcelain merely reflected public taste. The 1830s saw the latest rococo revival explode in a quite outrageous manner and all makers produced some pretty bizarre creations.

The Rockingham China Works was owned by the Brameld family and used premises on the estate of the Marquess of Rockingham, hence the name and the emblem of a heraldic griffin used as the factory's trade mark. The

first bone china was probably made in 1825. Earlier teasets and dessert services are elegant, often with a simple flower painted within a gold edge, but gradually fashion called for something more flamboyant. Even so, teacups in the form of bunches of primrose leaves must have taken some getting used to! Cup handles modelled as horse's legs, and teapot knops shaped as royal crowns somehow match elephant inkwells and a vase with a rhinoceros on the top, the latter of monumental proportion made to stand in a great hall.

It is easy to make fun of Rockingham, but these pieces are actually very well made, for the factory set it sights on the top rung of the English porcelain ladder. The award of an important royal order, a great dessert set made for William IV, gave Rockingham a major boost, but while

The soup tureen from a Rockingham armorial dinner service, 17in. (43cm), c.1828. The gnarled twig handles are typical of the factory's rustic designs.

putting all of their efforts into this one set, the management neglected common sense and failed to make enough profitable porcelain to keep the works going. Rockingham closed in 1842 although a small production was continued on the site by Isaac Baguley.

Rockingham has frequently suffered from its inferior china body that often crazed and stained, but plenty of surviving pieces do reflect the high ambitions of the management. Perfume bottles, baskets, desk sets, candlesticks and all sorts of miniature 'toys' can have painted scenes reserved on coloured backgrounds or applied modelled china flowers in the Dresden taste. A wide range of figures and animals was made, copying Derby or Continental prototypes and including a number of theatrical portraits. Many figures were sold in biscuit (or unglazed) versions which show the quality modelling, so often lost beneath Rockingham's thick glaze. Figures bear

impressed marks and model numbers. Teasets were marked usually only under the saucers. The factory mark was usually printed in red up until 1830 and in purple after this date with the addition of 'Manufacturers to the King', but there are many exceptions. A useful guide to attribution is the use of class numbers, the numerals 1 or 2 preceded by the abbreviation cl. usually painted in red on ornamental wares. Rockingham marks have often been imitated and fakes are still being made today. Rockingham shapes are pretty distinctive, however, and most can be checked with the standard reference books.

Further reading

Alwyn & Angela Cox, *Rockingham Pottery and Porcelain,* 1983

Denis Rice, *Rockingham Ornamental Porcelain,* 1965 and *Rockingham Pottery and Porcelain,* 1971

A simple Swansea porcelain vase probably painted by William Billingsley, c.1815. The vase leans heavily, having collapsed partly during the firing.

28. SWANSEA

While employed at Worcester from 1808, William Billingsley and Samuel Walker experimented to perfect a new kind of porcelain body. They left the employment of Barr, Flight and Barr suddenly in November 1813, taking with them the skills they had learnt, and after a short partnership with William Weston Young at Nantgarw, arrived in Swansea in 1814. With the backing of Lewis Dillwyn, Billingsley and Walker succeeded in making beautiful porcelain at the Cambrian works between 1814 and 1817.

The Swansea pastes range from a form of improved bone china to a superior glassy body resembling French hard paste porcelain. The various recipes attempted are all highly translucent, but were clearly very difficult to fire and kiln losses must have been heavy. Swansea was a failure from a financial point of view, but some truly wonderful porcelain was made, decorated in the elegant manner of the latest wares from Paris. Some Swansea porcelain was painted at the factory, by Billingsley and a number of highly talented decorators including Thomas Baxter. Other pieces were sent to London for decoration. The white porcelain was the most perfect background for painted flowers, but other forms of decoration include Japan patterns and coloured-in prints in Chinese taste.

In 1817 Dillwyn passed the running of the factory to Timothy and John Bevington who probably made very little porcelain after the departure of Billingsley and Walker who returned to Nantgarw in that year. Porcelain made at Swansea is frequently unmarked. Some pieces carry impressed marks, while others were marked in red enamel, either stencilled or painted with just the name Swansea. Attributing porcelain to Swansea is very difficult, even though the fine body should be distinctive. Similar shapes were made at Coalport after 1820 and a great deal of French porcelain, painted in London by the same decorators who painted on the Welsh china, has been incorrectly illustrated as Swansea in the past. Swansea's limited range of shapes are now well documented, however, and any attribution should be checked with recent reference books.

Further reading

W.D. John, *Swansea Porcelain,* 1958
P.E. Jones and Sir Leslie Joseph, *Swansea Porcelain, Shapes and Decoration,* 1989

29. NANTGARW

William Billingsley and Samuel Walker were at Nantgarw for less than a year from the end of 1813, during which time they probably experimented to perfect the porcelain made from the following year at Swansea. Any attribution to this first Nantgarw phase is doubtful and instead the porcelain we know to

This splendid Nantgarw plate was painted in London in the fashionable Continental taste, c.1820. 9¾in. (25cm), impressed NANT-GARW C.W.

have been made at Nantgarw was produced from 1817 until 1819, when Billingsley returned from Swansea.

Production largely consisted of plates and dishes, many of which had a moulded border pattern of ribbon-scrolls and leaves. Cabinet pieces such as small cups and saucers and desk sets were also made, as well as tea services and presentation cups for display rather than for use. The highly translucent body really does deserve its acclaim, and there was great demand from London china painters who were responsible for most of the richest forms of decoration. London-decorated dessert services are frequently assembled using Nantgarw plates but with French porcelain tureens or ice pails, for the Welsh porcelain proved particularly unreliable when hollow vessels were attempted— it simply melted out of shape in the kiln.

Some Nantgarw porcelain was painted at the factory in Wales, some by Billingsley himself with his distinctive roses. But, overcome by poverty, Billingsley departed for Coalport in 1819, leaving behind a failed venture. Thomas Pardoe decorated some of the remaining stock until 1822, while other pieces remained in the white or were subjected to almost amateur decoration many years later. Plates and dishes were marked with the neat impressed stamp NANT-GARW C.W., the initials thought to stand for China Works. Fakes exist, especially with the Nantgarw name mark added in enamels to genuine Coalport and other porcelain. All painted Nantgarw marks must be regarded as suspect, for this form of mark was basically not used at the time.

Further reading

W.D. John, *Nantgarw Porcelain,* 1948

Rowland Williams, *Nantgarw Porcelain 1813-1822,* 1993

Two fine Royal Worcester vases. Left, by John Stinton who specialised in painting Highland cattle, 14½in. (37cm), dated 1910. Right, by Thomas John Bott who learnt from his father the art of 'Limoges' style enamel, 12in. (30.5cm), dated 1881.

30. ROYAL WORCESTER

The enormous success afforded Royal Worcester in the nineteenth century is due to the endeavours of its Art Director, Richard William Binns. When Walter Chamberlain retired, the porcelain factory was managed by William Kerr and R.W. Binns who both came from retail backgrounds. They traded as Kerr and Binns for ten years until Kerr retired in

1862, leaving Binns in charge of a new company, the Worcester Royal Porcelain Co.

As soon as he arrived in 1852, Binns set about revitalising every aspect of the business. The old soaprock body was replaced by bone china, and a high quality Parian was introduced for busts and statues. Talented sculptors provided the models, especially a young Irishman, William Boyton Kirk. Figures had been a very small part of Worcester's market in

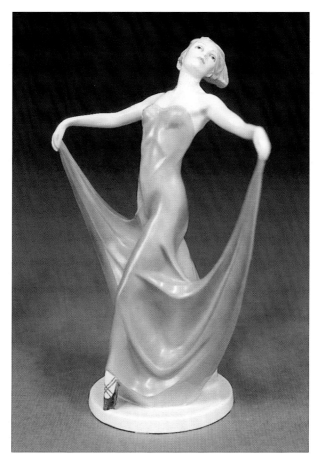

A Royal Worcester figure, 'Dance', by Doris Lindner issued in 1935. This was not a successful venture for the Worcester factory whose traditional customers did not understand Art Deco. 8½in. (21.5cm).   Private collection

the past, but within a few years Royal Worcester were the equal of Minton and Copeland, producing a wide range of figures, many of large size. The finest, and also the most commercial were modelled by James Hadley who gave life to the children in Kate Greenaway's book illustrations. Hadley's figures have great detail but retain a sculptural quality, emphasised by subtle decoration of gently shaded bronze and gold. Hadley was

able to model in any style, and quickly grasped the mood of Japanesque that swept Britain in the 1870s. R.W. Binns formed a personal collection of thousands of pieces of Oriental art, especially from Japan, displayed in his museum as inspiration for the factory craftsmen to create their own fantastic pieces. Vases were decorated with scenes from Japanese life, modelled by Hadley and carefully painted by James Callowhill. Figures of Indian craftsmen

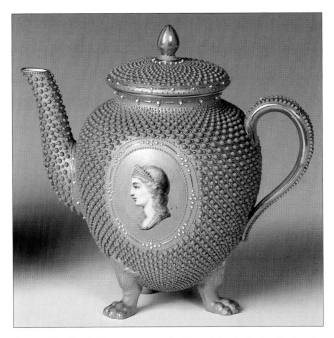

An exquisite Royal Worcester teapot by Samuel Ranford who developed a method of applying turquoise enamel to simulate jewels set in gold. 5¼in. (13.5cm) high, c.1875-77.

look as if they are made of ivory; indeed, at this period Royal Worcester seemed determined that its productions should not look like porcelain at all. Samuel Ranford produced jewelled work that seems to be made of pure gold. Thomas Bott and his son, Thomas John Bott, revived the ancient process of Limoges enamel, not on metal but on blue-glazed porcelain. The finest craftsman of all, George Owen, pierced Worcester vases into incredible networks of tiny holes, porcelain with the delicacy of Eastern ivory spheres. Worcester's imitation ivory vases, their shapes copied from Middle Eastern metal-work, were tremendously successful and sold all over the world. Valuable markets in the New World screamed out for Royal Worcester china, and Binns made sure his company occupied some of the biggest stands at exhibitions in Vienna, Paris, Chicago and Sydney.

Richard Binns and James Hadley both died in 1900 but while their passing marked the end of an era, their influence continued as some Hadley models remained in production until the 1960s. Ivory grounds remained popular until the 1920s, by which time the emphasis at Worcester had switched to fine free-hand painting. China shops now wanted signed works of art and Worcester found itself with a team of highly talented painters, each with their own subject at which they excelled. Walter Powell painted birds with an Art Nouveau mystique. Harry Davis painted a wide variety of landscapes including Highland scenes. James Stinton painted game birds, while his brother John painted Highland cattle on misty mountainsides. John's son, Harry Stinton continued his father's subject into the 1950s. Many artists painted studies of ripe fruit placed on mossy woodland banks, or luscious English roses, patterns that found widespread

A small loving cup in 'Old Derby' style, painted at the King Street factory by H.S. Hancock, 3in. (7.5cm) high, c.1910.

appeal. These pieces were expensive and during the 1920s sold in too few numbers to keep the factory going. Narrowly averting bankruptcy in 1930, Royal Worcester was saved once again by switching to figure making, following Doulton's lead. The charming children figurines of Freda Doughty and animals by Doris Lindner enabled Royal Worcester to recover its market position. Skills learnt at this time led to the creation of the incredible 'Doughty Birds', and other magnificent studies of horses, ladies in Victorian costume and tropical fish, issued during the 1960s and '70s as Limited Editions. Too costly to make any more, these later Royal Worcester pieces now re-sell for only a fraction of their manufacturing costs. A very great deal of Royal Worcester is available on the market today and it is necessary for collectors to specialise. At present nineteenth century figures offer possibly the best value around, but it is important to avoid restored examples.

Further reading

Richard Binns: *Worcester China 1852-1897,* 1897

Henry Sandon: *Royal Worcester Porcelain,* reprinted 1995

David, Henry and John Sandon, *The Sandon Guide to Royal Worcester Figures,* 1987

31. DERBY, THE KING STREET FACTORY

When the original Derby factory closed in 1848, a few former workmen made porcelain on a small scale in King Street in Derby. Their works were enlarged in 1862 under the management of George Stevenson and Sampson Hancock. To denote their partnership the old Derby red painted mark was revived with additional initials S and H added either side. All King Street porcelain tends to be referred to today as Stevenson and Hancock, but their partnership only lasted for four years. Instead from 1866 Hancock ran the works alone until his death in 1898 and so the S and H initials mostly refer to Sampson Hancock. Popular shapes and styles from the early nineteenth century were reproduced, especially the famous imari patterns. Figures such as the Mansion House Dwarfs and various theatrical subjects were also made, often cast from original Bloor Derby moulds (see page 124). The tiny letters S and H alongside the marks are sometimes the only clue to a late date, and it is hardly surprising that some specimens have been doctored by grinding away these initials to leave just the old Derby red mark. It is curious that, unlike most other makers after 1891, King Street marks never include the word England. Consequently most

Rich ground colours, lavish gilding with jewelled highlights and flower paintings by Désiré Leroy, Albert Gregory and Charles Harris. Royal Crown Derby at its most opulent.

King Street porcelain is claimed to be nineteenth century, even though the works continued until 1935. From 1917 the works were managed by William Larcombe and Francis Paget and the cipher WPL under the mark dates from this period. The Pagets eventually sold out to their great rivals Royal Crown Derby in 1935.

Further reading

Betty Bailey and John Twitchett, *Royal Crown Derby,* 1976

32. THE DERBY CROWN PORCELAIN CO. AND ROYAL CROWN DERBY

William Litherland and Edward Phillips left Royal Worcester in 1876 to establish a new china factory in Derby. Old Derby porcelain was popularly known as 'Crown Derby' and the name of the new company reflected this, for their intention was to reproduce the past in the same way as their rivals in King Street. The Derby Crown Porcelain Co. also made

ambitious new productions, however, some in the style of Royal Worcester. Raised-paste gilding was used on fancy vases and dessert services in Japanese or Middle-Eastern style, often with brightly coloured grounds.

The factory mark was two entwined Ds below a crown, printed in red or black. The company became Royal Crown Derby following the award of a Royal Warrant in 1890, although production continued without change. From 1882 an additional date code symbol was added below the mark, changing each year. From 1938 a simpler date code system commenced, using Roman numerals. I is 1938, XIII is 1950, XXIII is 1960 and so on.

Royal Crown Derby is best known for its imari patterns, copied from the Regency period. Collectors refer to the different imari designs by their pattern number, or use popular names such as 'Old Witches' and 'Cigar', called after the decorative bands which used to be wrapped around cigars. These patterns are still made by the company today.

Shelley are famous for their Art Deco coffee sets, the shapes and patterns combining together so wonderfully, c.1930.

From 1900-1930 an extensive range of miniature novelties were made in imari, including teasets, tiny mugs, kettles, milk churns and even a flat iron on its own trivet. Derby miniatures are highly collectable today. Derby's best work dates from early in the twentieth century, when vases and other ornamental shapes were cast with almost eggshell thinness. Decoration followed traditional French styles using rich ground colours. Many fine painters signed their work, including Albert Gregory and Cuthbert Gresley who painted delicate flowers and occasional landscapes. The greatest Derby artist, Désiré Leroy, was far more than just a skilled painter. As an all-round 'decorator', on pieces bearing his signature Leroy usually did the ground-laying, the painting, the jewelling, the gilding and the burnishing. His death in 1908 marked the end of an era, for no artist since has come close to equalling his craftsmanship and skill.

Further reading

Betty Bailey and John Twitchett, *Royal Crown Derby*, 1976

33. SHELLEY

James Wileman and Co. operated the Foley pottery in Fenton, Staffordshire, specialising in good, everyday teawares. The factory's history is confusing as other local china makers also used the name Foley and Foley China. Joseph Shelley became Wileman's partner in 1872 and manager from 1884. His son, Percy Shelley continued the business after 1896. The Wileman name was retained until 1925 when the firm traded as Shelleys, and as Shelley Potteries Ltd. from 1929. Pottery was also made, and some distinctive vases, but it is as a maker of bone china teasets that Shelley has become famous. Wileman period designs are very traditional, supplying the general public with usable sets that are generally unexciting. During the 1920s, however, the firm discovered Art Deco and became an important maker of the most fashionable china of the day. The china shops of 1930 displayed affordable Shelley teasets in a wide range of patterns and stylish shapes, including square cups and triangular handles. Some designs are reasonably tame, with printed flowers or painted landscapes. Others are imaginative, with coloured bands and stripes, spots or intersecting geometric shapes. Some designs include bright platinum lustre. Shelley teasets are always well made and are generally reasonably priced today. Shelleys were taken over by Royal Doulton in 1971.

Further reading
W. Harvey, C. Watkins and R. Senft, *Shelley Potteries,* 1980

---

34. MOORE BROTHERS AND BERNARD MOORE

Bernard and Samuel Moore succeeded their father at his china works in Longton in about 1872, making traditional teasets and tableware, but the Moore brothers achieved fame for their distinctive ornaments produced during the 1880s and early 1890s. Dresden was the inspiration for centrepieces modelled with Cupids supporting water lily leaves, flowering cacti and globes adorned with modelled grapes or hops. Mostly issued just in white bone china with limited colouring and gilded bases,

A model of a monkey by Bernard Moore, the master ceramicist who showed such wonderful control over Flambé glazes, c.1900.   Private collection

Moore Brothers porcelain was inexpensive and popular. Although highly decorative and keenly collected, Moore's inferior china body has not stood the test of time very well and examples can be badly cracked or discoloured.

During the 1890s Bernard Moore became increasingly interested in ceramic glazes and Moore Brothers porcelain animals were decorated with curious flambés and other brightly coloured glazes. When the Longton works closed in 1905, Bernard Moore moved to Stoke-on-Trent where he worked as a decorator rather than as a china maker. Bone china and earthenware 'blanks' were bought from several manufacturers including Wedgwood, Minton and Royal Worcester and decorated with flambé and lustre finishes, some of which can be very beautiful. Moore Brothers porcelain is usually marked with their name impressed, while pieces decorated by Bernard Moore are signed in full or bear just his initials BM. He continued as a decorator into the 1920s and died in 1935.

Further reading
Victoria and Albert Museum Catalogue, *Bernard Moore, Master Potter,* 1982

---

35. DOULTON

Henry Doulton operated a vast and successful stoneware factory in Lambeth but, while clearly a potter at heart, he also desired to make porcelain. He realised there were no china-making traditions in Lambeth and instead took over a Staffordshire pottery factory and commenced his own porcelain in Burslem in 1883. As newcomers in the area of fine porcelain, Doulton were able to look at the work of established firms and attracted some of the most talented artists working for their competitors. Foremost among these was Charles Noke, a sculptor with a great interest in ceramic technology. Noke had trained at Worcester under James Hadley and his early figure models at Burslem follow the formal traditions of Worcester. Under Noke's direction Doulton put on a most impressive display at the Chicago Exhibition in 1893, including large freely

The influence of Japan is seen in this Doulton Flambé glazed vase of c.1905.

painted vases. Doulton's bone china, with rich painting and raised gilding, was as accomplished as any from Minton or Worcester, but the best Burslem pieces are neglected today as collectors still associate Doulton with heavy pottery. Working with Harry Nixon, Charles Noke developed some wonderful glazes both for pottery and porcelain. 'Titanian' used delicate porcelain stained with subtle colours in an attempt to reproduce the work of chemists at Copenhagen and Meissen. Doulton's Flambé ware enjoyed far greater colour control than Bernard Moore ever achieved in Stoke-on-Trent, while other glazes sparkled with living crystals or imitated Eastern 'Jade' with a curious beauty. The Burslem factory was enlarged in 1907 when production reached staggering

Charles Noke developed many exciting glazes at Doulton. This is his 'Jade' glaze, used on a tiny dog group, c.1925.

Doulton's delightful crinoline ladies enjoy continued popularity. These charming subjects sold in great numbers and most are common today, while certain rarities, in short production, can be surprisingly valuable.

proportions. Profits came from everyday teasets and cheap ornaments, such as the 'Blue Children' range which used a combination of painting and printing, and commemorative Jubilee and Coronation beakers made in unbelievable quantities. These subsidised the ambitious 'exhibition pieces', massive vases painted by the top artists which heaped great praise on the company. Doulton followed fashion more closely than other major British porcelain firms. Consequently in the 1920s and '30s Doulton made exciting Art Deco teasets alongside totally modern sculpture. Doulton porcelain is associated in most people's minds with its extensive range of figurines and character jugs. C.J. Noke began figure making at Burslem in the 1880s but it was not until 1913, when Queen Mary admired a selection of small figures on show at the factory, that figure making was greatly extended. Some figures were the work of free-lance designers such as Charles Vyse and Phoebe Stabler. Most were conceived and modelled by the factory's own sculptors such as Leslie Harradine, Harry Tittensor and

Peggy Davis who understood precisely the subjects that sold best. Today the Old Balloon Lady and girls in colourful crinolines sit on mantelpieces in every country, giving enormous pleasure to new generations. The most attractive figures sold well and these tend to be the least valuable, while the curious oddities that struggled to find customers during the Depression years can be worth incredible sums to keen collectors today. Careful marketing and a thriving Collectors' Club have elevated Doulton to the rank of probably the most widely collected of all English porcelain makers, a position they very much deserve. Virtually all Doulton porcelain is marked, usually with the firm's printed emblem, while date codes using clear numbers are stamped into many pieces also.

Further reading
Desmond Eyles: *The Doulton Burslem Wares,* 1980
Desmond Eyles and Richard Dennis, *Royal Doulton Figures,* 1978, revised 1987
The Lyle Price Guide to Doulton, 1986 et al

A Royal Doulton jester modelled by Charles Noke and produced c.1928. This example is a rare colour variation and sold in 1995 for £5,060, whereas the more usual, colourful version sells for between £600 and £800.

CHAPTER 12

The Rest of the World

INTRODUCTION

The vast majority of the world's porcelain was produced in the six countries previously discussed. Absence of technical know-how or suitable raw materials prevented other kings and countries realising their own dreams of porcelain manufacture, mainly because a suitable source of kaolin could not be discovered. In Russia Peter the Great sent envoys to Peking to discover the secret of porcelain but without success, and it was not until his daughter the Empress Elisabeth engaged defectors from Meissen that any porcelain could be made in Russia. In America experiments by Andrew Duché to make porcelain with clay from Savannah were a failure, as was the venture by Bonnin and Morris in Philadelphia. The great continent of America had to rely on imported European and Oriental porcelain, in the absence of any really successful porcelain of their own. Irish potters who made porcelain at Belleek emigrated to America where a similar artificial porcelain was made, but it was never a commercial success. For all its size and mineral wealth, porcelain clay was never discovered in Australia. The first settlers sent back stoneware clay from Sydney Cove to be fired at Wedgwood's factory in Staffordshire, but this did not lead to any successful Australian ceramic factory. Consequently antipodean porcelain is limited to a few china painters who decorated Limoges blanks. Africa, India, and, more surprisingly, the Middle East, all lacked the ability to make successful porcelain.

In this section are discussed the principal European porcelain factories which fall outside Germany, France, Italy and Britain. Some, like Copenhagen, were major manufacturers, while others were unimportant to the history of porcelain in terms of their size. It is natural for collectors to want to buy the products of their own nations, however, and so it is hardly surprising Zürich and Nyon porcelain is worth a great deal more than the teawares of similar quality made by small Parisian china makers. Room prevents any discussion of the porcelains made at Vista Alegre in Portugal, Alcora in Spain, Marieburg in Sweden, and other similar ventures, and instead a few of the larger producers are discussed together, country by country.

1. UNITED STATES OF AMERICA

Early settlers discovered white clay and hoped to establish an American porcelain industry. Andrew Duché experimented in Savannah, Georgia and as early as 1738 claimed to have made 'a small teacup... [which] when held against the Light, was very near transparent'. Duché may have exaggerated, for this was still long before the first English porcelain and certainly none of Duché's porcelain survives. However, his experiments with American clay probably aided the establishment of a porcelain factory in Philadelphia by Gousse Bonnin and George Morris in 1770. Blue and white soft-paste porcelain closely resembles Bow in shape and decoration, for workmen came from England to make the open baskets, shell pickle stands and rococo sauceboats, identified by the rare mark of a letter P or through matching shards excavated in Philadelphia. The Bonnin and Morris factory lasted less than three years and examples are amongst the most valuable porcelain in the world today – through rarity rather than merit.

Early nineteenth century American porcelain resembles Bohemian or Limoges to the extent that most cannot be identified, for factory marks were rarely used. Two Frenchmen, Louis Decasse and Nicolas Chanou, made teasets in New York from c.1824 and the few known pieces are superbly gilded. Sadly the

'American Belleek' at its most flamboyant. This pot-pourri vase was made c.1880 at Trenton, New Jersey by the firm of Ott and Brewer. Marked 'Belleek' under the base, this piece is far removed in taste from its Irish heritage. 13½in. (34cm). Sotheby's, New York

A fine vase of Limoges porcelain painted in the Lingquist Art Shop in Chicago, 13¼in. (34cm), dated 1915. China painters all over America used Limoges porcelain in the absence of locally produced porcelain blanks. Sandon collection

works were destroyed by fire in 1827. Not far away in New Jersey, William Shirley also used French-trained craftsmen and contemporary accounts describe his fine porcelain. Sadly all that survives is a single plain bowl. Far more is known about the porcelain made by the Tucker family in Philadelphia who owned a china store and began by decorating imported white porcelain. In 1826 William Tucker opened his own factory reproducing the kind of wares he had previously sold. Vases can be identified by primitive paintings of Philadelphian land-marks, for Tucker porcelain has the quaint charm of a provincial French or Staffordshire factory. Pieces can only be attributed to early American makers if they *exactly* match the shape of documentary wares. A lot of jugs and

vases sold today in American shops as 'probably Tucker' are in reality French.

In the mid-nineteenth century the most important American makers were Charles Cartlidge & Co. and the Union Porcelain Works at Greenpoint, New York; and the United States Pottery Co. of Bennington, Vermont. Bennington is famous for relief-moulded jugs and models of poodles, but, because so much has been incorrectly attributed to Bennington, any ascription simply has to be supported by expert opinion. Some Cartlidge pieces are much easier to identify, for jugs were proudly moulded with American eagles and flags.

Trenton, New Jersey, became the centre of the American porcelain industry. Parian was

A pair of American porcelain pitchers by Tucker and Hulme, made in Philadelphia in 1828. While attributions to Tucker can be controversial, these can be identified with certainty by painted name marks underneath. 9½in. (24cm) high.   Sotheby's, New York

the important new material in England and it was soon discovered local clay produced excellent parian at Trenton. It was here that the firm of Ott and Brewer produced their copies of Belleek and Royal Worcester, and the most famous American parian – a series of figures playing baseball – was modelled by Isaac Broome for Ott and Brewer in 1875. The same sculptor also modelled busts of Washington, Lincoln and other American notables. The delicate glazed parian made at Belleek in Ireland was well received in America and copies were soon being made. Ott and Brewer introduced their eggshell porcelain in 1882, aided by workmen who came from the Belleek

factory. The Willets Manufacturing Co. in Trenton also employed Irish potters and nobody questioned the right of these American factories to call their porcelain 'Belleek'. Many products copy Irish Belleek exactly. Others used the thin, iridescent material for more original shapes inspired by Japan.

Walter Scott Lenox worked first for Ott and Brewer and then for Willets before starting his own porcelain firm in 1889, in partnership with Jonathan Coxon. His Ceramic Art Company made a creamy Belleek-like glazed parian decorated in a more original manner. Fine painting and gilding was executed in the manner of Worcester and Vienna by artists

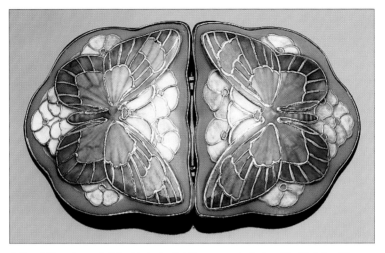

A Royal Copenhagen belt buckle in the Art Nouveau taste designed by Christian Thomsen in 1905.

including Lucien Boullemier who came from Minton. Lenox even employed two Japanese artists in the 1890s, for *Japanesque* designs were still popular. Tiffany & Co. in New York sold Lenox and other Trenton and New York porcelain alongside Limoges china decorated in America by independent painters. China painting was a popular pastime all across America and the results range from highly competent to decidedly amateur.

A very different kind of porcelain, original and very modern, was made in America from c.1900. The former Sèvres artist, Taxile Doat, was joined at his pottery in University City, Missouri in 1910 by a talented American lady, Adelaide Robineau, who had worked previously at Syracuse, New York. Coloured clays and crystalline glazes were put to incredible use, creating ceramic vases to rival the best French and Austrian art pottery. Although the Lenox factory continued, twentieth century American porcelain remained individual and was produced only on a small scale.

Further reading

Alice Cooney Frelinghuysen, *American Porcelain,* 1989

DENMARK

Porcelain manufacture was attempted in Copenhagen by Christoph Hunger early in the eighteenth century, and a Frenchman, Louis Fournier came from Vincennes and Chantilly c.1760-65 but his soft-paste manufactory also failed. The Royal Copenhagen factory was founded by Frantz Müller early in the 1770s under the patronage of the Queen, but only achieved success after the King bought the factory in 1779. The taste at that time was Classical and early Copenhagen follows tradition with careful landscape and flower painting. A speciality of the factory was painted silhouette portraits. The celebrated 'Flora Danica' dinner service was commissioned in 1789 as an intended gift for Catherine II of Russia, but it took so long for the painter J.C. Bayer to complete the different botanical paintings that Catherine died before the gift could be presented. The set was finally completed in 1802 and the Danish court decided to keep it. Reproductions of the Flora Danica set were made in the twentieth century.

Some fine landscape painting and grand presentation vases were made during the

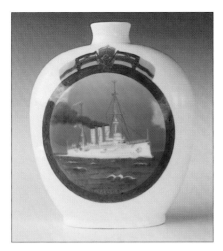

The Emden, *a German warship, painted in typical colours, c.1905-10. Royal Copenhagen specialised in plain vase shapes that did not clash with the painted decoration.*

ninctccnth century but generally Copenhagen porcelain declined. Ordinary tea services with simple blue and white patterns were made in large numbers along with copies of Meissen flower painting on tablewares. High quality biscuit figures after the sculptor Thorwaldsen were very successful judging by the numbers surviving today, especially circular biscuit roundels. These are often marked with the word Eneret which simply means registered. The factory was purchased by Philip Schou c.1883 and the works were moved to the site of his previous earthenware factory. Schou appointed Arnold Krog as Art Director and his skills as a ceramicist quickly reversed the firm's dwindling fortunes. Krog introduced a new style of free-hand painting in high-temperature underglaze colours inspired by the latest Fukagawa porcelain from Japan, although patterns were more European. The result was an original form of art porcelain which was soon copied all over Europe, and at Meissen in particular. The soft blue colouring was used for the first of a long series of annual calendar plates, early examples of which have a unique beauty, but these are neglected today due to the disastrous state of the market in 'Collectors' Plates'. During the 1890s some quite remarkable glaze effects were created at Copenhagen by the chemist Valdemar Engelhardt, used on plain vase shapes to great

acclaim. Copenhagen figure and animal models were the most original in Europe, naturalistic and yet gently stylised. Modellers included Knud Kyhn, Jais Neilsen and Christian Thomsen who mastered his own gentle Art Nouveau. Since the eighteenth century Copenhagen porcelain has been marked with three wavy lines in blue. A crown was added after 1880 with the word Denmark and Royal Copenhagen used in the twentieth century.

During the 1850s a new factory was established in Copenhagen by local china dealers the Bing brothers and a modeller from the Royal factory, F. Grondahl. Bing and Grondahl mostly follow the precise styles made popular at their rival Royal factory, although some original designs were made. Their finest achievement was the so-called 'Heron Service' modelled with Japanese-like birds by Pietro Krohn.

Finally mention should be made of porcelain punchbowls and plates associated with the port of Elsinor. These were probably manufactured in Copenhagen but there was a tradition of ship painting in Elsinor and during the later nineteenth century visiting vessels were copied on to 'Elsinor Bowls' as presentation pieces for the ship's officers.

Further reading

H.V.F. Winstone, *Royal Copenhagen,* 1984

A Loosdrecht teabowl and saucer, c.1775, painted with a simple elegance that typifies Dutch porcelain, marked M.o.L.

3. HOLLAND

Count Gronsveldt-Diepenbroek bought the Weesp porcelain factory in 1759 and made true porcelain in the Meissen style, although Dutch porcelain was much gentler in design and colouring than contemporary German. In 1771 the factory was sold to J. de Mol who moved the works to Oude Loosdrecht. The factory specialised in elegant tewares with flower or landscape painting often in a single colour. A few figures were modelled by Nicolas Gauron who came from Tournai. The mark M.o.L was used for Manufacture Oude Loosdrecht but the same letters spelt the name of the owner. On de Mol's death in 1782 the factory was moved once again to Amstel where porcelain was made until 1820. Amstel porcelain was influenced by contemporary French and marked examples are rare.

At The Hague a decorating establishment was run by Johann Lyncker and his father, from 1776-1790. A small amount of hard paste porcelain was made here, but mostly white porcelain was bought from Tournai and from Ansbach in Germany for painting at The Hague. The soft, creamy paste of Tournai was well suited to the gentle flower painting and exotic bird decoration which was a speciality, as well as monochrome landscapes. The mark was the sign of The Hague, a stork in blue, sometimes painted on top of the A mark of Ansbach.

At the very end of the nineteenth century an architect, Juriaan Kok, took over a small pottery at Rozenburg near The Hague and introduced a frit porcelain which could be moulded and fired extremely thin. Rozenburg 'eggshell' was made between 1899 and 1913 and is one of the most original forms of European porcelain. The

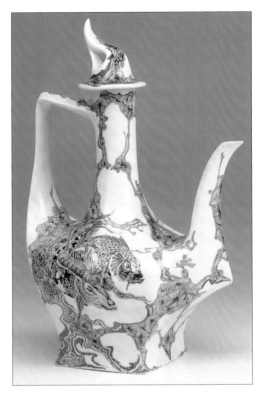

*A Rozenburg 'eggshell' porcelain coffee pot, the exciting
decoration mirroring the ingenuity of the shape, c.1900.*
Peter Oosthuizen

shapes were angular and yet natural, suited to
the Dutch taste in Art Nouveau. The very
different style of painting was derived from the
patterns seen on Javanese batik brought back
from the old Dutch East Indies, featuring fine
delineation in colours and shading with tiny dots.
Artists such as S. Schellink signed their work
which comprised flowers, leaves, birds and
spiders' webs. The mark was once again the stork
of The Hague but with the name of Rozenburg in
addition, a name keenly collected today.

Further reading
Haags Gemeentemuseum Exhibition Catalogue
1983, *Rozenburg 1883-1917*

4. IRELAND

Irish porcelain means basically just one thing –
Belleek. For a special exhibit at the 1853 Dublin
exhibition, Kerr and Binns of Worcester had
used Irish clay and Irish gold. Their experiments
came to the attention of David McBirney and
R.W. Armstrong who hoped to establish a new
industry in Ireland. A factory was constructed at
Belleek, near Enniskillen in Co. Fermanagh and
the first porcelain was probably on sale in 1863.
Initially Belleek made a form of bone china, but
this was soon replaced by parian, delicate and
thin with a glaze the colour of ivory. Belleek
porcelain could be moulded to an eggshell

Belleek porcelain is famous for its seashell shapes, eggshell thinness and mother-of-pearl lustre glaze, all represented by this 'Marine' centrepiece, 11½in. (29cm), c.1900.

thinness with all the delicacy of a seashell, and so it is hardly surprising shells and other marine life dominated the shapes of Belleek china. Teasets were given the names of shells – *Tridacna, Echidna* and *Neptune*, and the shiny white glaze was sometimes given a mother-of-pearl lustre. Dainty teawares were gently edged in pink or green but, apart from a few shamrock leaves or wild grasses heightened in enamels, virtually no other painting was employed at the Belleek factory. The 'Prince of Wales Service' typifies the Belleek style, with merboys and Tritons supporting shells embossed with coral and bulrushes.

Belleek made a small range of parian busts and figures but these were unsuccessful and are rare today. Belleek is best known for its baskets made of delicate woven strands of porcelain. Some are further adorned with incredible china flowers, every petal applied with precision. Collectors look for earlier examples where the basketweave centres were formed of three-ply plaited strands, as 'four-strand' centres indicate a twentieth century date. It is often said that the quality of Belleek declined after Armstrong's death in 1884, when the firm became The Belleek Pottery Co., but this is simply not true. Very few new shapes were introduced, but new designs were unnecessary – Belleek could sell as much fine porcelain as it could make. In truth the only way to tell a later Belleek product is the form and colour of the factory trade mark. Three important emblems of Ireland – a harp, a tower and a wolfhound – were printed in black or impressed from c.1863, usually above the name Belleek. Additional words 'Co. Fermanagh, Ireland' were added in 1891 giving rise to what collectors term the 'Second Period' of the factory. In 1927 a further addition to the factory mark was a round Celtic emblem with the words *Deanta in Eirinn* which means simply 'Made in Ireland'. After World War II the mark was printed in green instead of black, and the sign of a letter R in a circle indicates a date after 1955. Belleek is still made today in a tradition unchanged since the 1860s.

Further reading
Richard K. Dagenhardt, *Belleek*, 2nd edition, 1993
Marion Langham, *Belleek Irish Porcelain*, 1993

5. KOREA

The earliest porcelain made in Korea naturally followed Chinese styles although somewhat individual celadon was made datable to the tenth century. Some twelfth century Korean porcelain is not much inferior to Chinese *Qingbai* and interesting inlaid decoration occurs on Korean celadon also from the twelfth century. This inlay is often in black and white clay applied with great subtlety. Blue and white was first made for King Sejo (1456-68) as copies of gifts he had received from China, but, under orders from the Court, blue and white was only made for the Korean Royal household up until the late sixteenth century when Korea was overrun by the Japanese. Korean potters were forced to go to Japan and set up kilns near Arita, and in the turbulent history that followed there was no significant porcelain industry remaining in Korea.

Gradually blue and white was reintroduced in the seventeenth century and splendid jars were painted with dragons which have a cartoon-like freedom lacking in their more refined Chinese

A Korean vase from the Yi dynasty, 18th/19th century, 10½in. (27cm). This typical primitive decoration is highly regarded today.

counterparts. Some curiously beautiful white porcelain brushpots with pierced decoration were made in the eighteenth century, but generally Korean ceramics from the latter part of the Yi dynasty in the eighteenth and nineteenth centuries appear crude and primitive. While lacking in artistry to the uninitiated, the handmade quality of Korean porcelain appeals to the Oriental eye. Sombre and austere, it possesses 'quiet beauty' much appreciated by Eastern collectors, for in recent years some exceptional prices have been paid for some specimens offered for sale in the West.

Further reading
Itoh Ikutaroh, et al., *Korean Ceramics from the Ataka Collection*, 1992
Chewon Kim & G. Gompertz, *The Ceramic Art of Korea*, 1961

A selection of porcelain Easter eggs, given as presents all over Russia in the 19th century and popular collectors' items today.

6. RUSSIA

Most people think only of porcelain Easter eggs, but in addition to these special pieces made for the Tsars, Russian factories have made porcelain in the style of every other part of Europe. Peter the Great's daughter, the Empress Elisabeth, wanted a china factory of her own and in 1744 engaged Christoph Hunger, formerly of Meissen and Vienna, who claimed to know the secret processes. It is said Hunger produced only a dozen misshapen cups, and after three years he was replaced by the son of a Russian priest, Dmitri Vinogradov. His experiments were successful, but because of his excessive drinking, the director of the porcelain factory, Baron Cherkassov, ordered Vinogradov to be imprisoned in chains and

A collection of 19th century Russian figures including examples from the Gardner, Kuznetsov and Popov factories, the large Cossack 10½in. (27cm).

made him write down every recipe and process, the Baron's cruel behaviour ensuring the continuation of the porcelain factory.

Catherine II kept a close personal interest in the factory and attracted skilled potters from the leading factories of Europe. Early Russian imperial porcelain shows the influence of Meissen, but Catherine also encouraged native Russian traditions. In 1779 the Imperial factory engaged a sculptor from Copenhagen, Jean Rachette, to model figurines in Russian regional costumes, in the manner of Kändler at Meissen. Rachette's typical Russian peasants and tradesmen began a tradition which was followed by other Russian factories, notably that of the Gardner family. Early Gardner porcelain has a German feel, but commissions from the Empress Catherine introduced Russian themes into Gardner figures in particular. Mostly the private factories took inspiration for their tableware from foreign china, as Nicholas I had placed a heavy tariff on all imported porcelain. The factories of Popov, Kornilov and Kuznetsov

accounted for an enormous decorative output, much of it mirroring European wares from Paris or Bohemia.

One feature of Russian porcelain is the bright coloured grounds, in brilliant blue or green enamel, sometimes semi-matt; also a dark chocolate brown, bold red or crimson, each emphasised by very bright gilding. These same colours appear on the costumes of Russian figures and conjure up images of malachite and lapis lazuli. Trading links with England meant that Russian porcelain could be bought readily in London. The Imperial factory's display at the 1851 Great Exhibition was well received and typically Russian figures can be found in many British families. The Crimean War interrupted this trade and led the Russian porcelain industry into decline. The emancipation of the serfs in 1861 deprived the private porcelain factories of their cheap, almost slave labour, and only the biggest makers survived by looking to new markets with cheap mass-production aimed at Asia and the Middle East. These inexpensive

A pair of Imperial porcelain vases with impressive ormolu mounts, made for the palace of the Grand Duke Alexander Alexandrovich (later Alexander III), 28¼in. (72cm), c.1890.

products are common today and give Russian porcelain a somewhat unwarranted reputation for cheap vulgarity.

Alexander II allowed the Imperial factory to deteriorate, but his wife the Empress halted the decline by sending the factory's senior modeller to England to bring back specimens of modern porcelain to be copied. Her son, Tsar Alexander III, transformed the factory during the 1880s,

with special orders for his court which were elegant but mostly plain, the Raphael Service being an ambitious exception, based on copies of Raphael's Vatican frescos on the walls of the Hermitage. Nicholas II and Alexandra had little interest in porcelain, preferring instead the work of the Imperial jewellers.

The Revolution marked the end of Russian porcelain in one sense, but a new beginning in

An Imperial porcelain plate with military decoration painted by N. Yakovlev, dated 1840, 9½in. (24cm), part of an important service made for Nicholas I.

another. Old white porcelain, stored at the Imperial factory, was decorated in the 1920s with portraits of Lenin and symbols of the Soviet Republic in the splendid new style of *agitprop*. Some of these pieces can be very expensive today, but beware of clever copies, recently made in Russia to trick unsuspecting tourists. Modern Russian porcelain factories make pleasant examples of folk craft, and an extensive series of porcelain animals which have become highly collectable in recent years.

Further reading

Richard Hare, *Art and Artists of Russia*
Marvin Ross, *Russian Porcelains,* 1968
N.I. Rostovsky, *Revolutionary Ceramics,* 1990

7. SWITZERLAND

In terms of originality, the porcelain made at Zürich and Nyon is far from remarkable, but its rarity value means it is keenly collected in present day Switzerland. Firstly faience and then an experimental soft paste porcelain were made at Schoren, near Zürich, but it is the true porcelain made from 1765 under the direction of A. Spengler that has achieved notoriety. It is appropriate geographically that Zürich porcelain should combine German and French influences. Meissen style flower painting in colours and underglaze blue was made alongside delicate landscape painting which is closer in feel to French faience. Plain coloured rims with little or no gilding are subtle but unexciting. In contrast

A selection of Nyon porcelain decorated with characteristic elegance, all marked with a fish in blue, c.1780-90.   Phillips, Geneva

Zürich figures can be delightful. Most were modelled by J.V. Sonnenschein who came from Ludwigsburg and indeed, these two factory's productions are easily confused for Zürich figures are often unmarked. The mark of a letter Z in blue is usually large and clear on tea and dinner wares, however.

Nyon porcelain was made under the direction of J. Dortu and F. Müller who is believed to have learnt his skills at Frankenthal. Production commenced c.1780 by which time the principal influences in Switzerland came from Paris. Without the blue-painted mark of a fish it would be almost impossible to distinguish Nyon teawares from those made by smaller French factories, delightful but very simple with coloured border patterns or scattered sprigs. Because both of these Swiss porcelain factories were short-lived, there were already many collectors by the late nineteenth century. Consequently Samson saw a ready market for clever fakes and his versions of the Z and fish marks are often encountered. It is easy to assume the great French copyist would not have bothered with such simple patterns, and consequently Samson fakes are regularly offered for sale as genuine productions of Nyon and Zürich.

A Zürich needle case or etui in the shape of a Wickelkind, a delightful gift for a new mother, 3¼in. (8.2cm), c.1780.

Marks and Guides to Dating

The Chinese invented porcelain marks, not to tell who made a pot but to identify the Ming Emperor who placed the order. Many reigns later, new Emperors demanded copies complete with false marks, to show that the skill which created the Ming originals still existed. The Qing Emperors were no doubt impressed, but while their potters strived to reproduce the legendary Ming 'heaping and piling', they learnt that the easiest part to copy was the mark of their illustrious forebears.

In Europe marks are an essential guide to identification. Factory marks were placed on porcelain to publicise the makers, but, curiously, full names were hardly ever used in the eighteenth century. Instead the marks that have become legendary are the emblems of Principalities or the initial ciphers of the factory owners. The crossed swords of Meissen were derived from the arms of Saxony, while Sèvres used the Royal cipher of King Louis XV, but we can only speculate as to why Chelsea used an anchor. European makers regularly copied each other and thought nothing of imitating rival factory marks. Fakes abound, and this is why experts will tell you that the mark is the last thing they look at to judge the authenticity of a piece of eighteenth century porcelain

Nineteenth century factories faced much greater competition and this is why full names or at least the initials of makers were now used as standard, printed or impressed on the bases of all their products. China retailers did not approve of factory marks, as they wanted customers to return to their shops when placing further orders. Consequently factories which had their own shops usually marked their porcelain, while smaller makers who relied on general china dealers were prevented from signing their wares – a pattern number was sufficient to allow china shops to re-order from the makers. Some factories added the name of the retailer to their porcelain and it is easy to confuse a dealer's name with that of the maker: Thomas Goode & Co. of London, Donovan of Dublin, Tiffany of New York, Bailey, Banks and Biddle of Philadelphia. The names of these big china shops are better known to collectors than many a manufacturer.

Factory marks and retailer's names are not the only marks which appear on porcelain. For the purposes of copyright, various forms of registration marks were used. Geschultz, Deposé and Eneret are often incorrectly listed as makers, but these names which appear on porcelain simply translate as 'Registered' in German, French and Danish. From 1842 a diamond-shaped symbol was used in England with code letters giving the day, month and year a design was first registered. Specialist mark books can identify who patented certain designs, while others can be identified by contacting the Design Registration Office at Kew in south-west London. From 1884 a single Registration number replaced the diamond mark and this gives the year a design was registered (although not necessarily when it was made).

Date codes often occur on porcelain from the later nineteenth century. Their purpose was to tell makers how long undecorated stock had been stored in a factory, partly to prevent old wares burning when they were re-fired. Date marks are, of course, most helpful to collectors today. Sèvres, Berlin and Worcester used simple alphabet codes, while Minton and Derby used geometric symbols which can be looked up in specialist books. Many factories including Sèvres, Vienna, Coalport and Doulton impressed or incised the day, month and year into the base of many products, although not every number stamped into a piece of porcelain indicates the date it was made. Shape, model and pattern numbers were used between makers and their china shops and these link up to factory records, some of which still survive in larger archives. Most factories used complicated workmen's marks to identify the potters and decorators responsible, so that the craftsmen could be paid at the end of the week. Some artists at certain factories can be identified, as well as independent artist potters who stamped their own initials into their creation, but most workmen's marks are just meaningless codes today.

The Mckinley Tariff Act of 1891 required all goods imported into the United States to bear the name of the country of origin in English. Porcelain makers around the world amended their marks to include the country name, so that pieces marked 'England', 'Germany' or 'Japan' in English will always date from 1891 or later. 'Made in England' will date from either 1900 or 1926, although not every maker or country adopted the 'Made in…' slogan. It must be remembered, however, that the regulations only applied to goods exported to America. Most firms amended all of their marks anyway, but pieces produced for the home market did not always state their country on them. Do not assume, therefore, that a piece without the word 'England' on it has to be older than 1891.

Painted mark

Six character reign mark of the emperor Jiajing, painted in underglaze blue, Chinese Ming dynasty, 1522-66.

Painted mark

Derby painted mark (crown, cross and D) with additional letters S H representing Sampson Hancock of the King Street factory, c.1900.

Painted mark

Hunting horn in red enamel, Chantilly factory, France, c.1735.

Seal mark

Imperial seal mark of the Emperor Jiaqing, on a wucai 'Dragon and Phoenix' bowl, 1796-1820.

Seal mark

The signature Kozan on a Meiji period teapot from the Japanese workshop of Makuzu Kozan, late 19th century.

Printed mark

Royal Worcester's mark for 1872, including the numeral 51 for the date of the factory's founding in 1751.

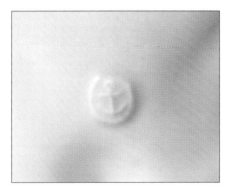

Embossed mark

The raised anchor mark of Chelsea, on a small pad of clay, c.1750.

Workmen's mark

The Sèvres factory mark (the cipher of King Louis XVI) with date letter ee for 1782, the painter's mark of Vincent Taillandier and the gilder's mark of Michel-Barnabe Chauveaux.

Impressed mark

Miles Mason's name mark clearly impressed on a plate, c.1805-10.

Fake mark

The AR cipher for Augustus Rex, used at Meissen under Augustus the Strong, c.1725-30, but here used by Helena Wolfsohn in Dresden, c.1870.

Chinese Dynasties and Periods

Tang Dynasty	618-906	Jiajing	1522-1566
		Longqing	1567-1572
Five Dynasties	907-960	Wanli	1573-1619
		Tianqi	1621-1627
Song Dynasty		Chongzhen	1628-1643
Northern	960-1127		
Southern	1128-1279	**Qing Dynasty**	
		Shunzi	1644-1661
Yuan Dynasty	1279-1368	Kangxi	1662-1722
		Yongzheng	1723-1735
Ming Dynasty		Qianlong	1736-1795
Hongwu	1368-1398	Jiaqing	1796-1820
Yongle	1403-1424	Daoguang	1821-1850
Xuande	1426-1435	Xianfeng	1851-1861
Chenghua	1465-1487	Tongzhi	1862-1874
Hongzhi	1488-1505	Guangxu	1875-1908
Zhengde	1506-1521	Xuantong	1909-1912

Selected Bibliography

This list contains titles of general books on porcelain. Books covering specific subjects are listed in the appropriate chapter. All are recommended reading, although many are now out of print and difficult to obtain.

Mark Books

William Chaffers: *Marks and Monograms on Pottery & Porcelain,* 15th revised edition, Reeves, 1974

John Cushion: *Handbook of Pottery and Porcelain Marks,* Faber & Faber, 1980, revised edition 1996

Danckert: *Directory of European Porcelain,* NAG Press, 1981

Geoffrey A. Godden: *Encyclopaedia of British Pottery and Porcelain Marks,* Barrie & Jenkins, several editions

General Books (World)

David Battie (Ed.): *Sotheby's Concise Encyclopedia of Porcelain,* Conran Octopus, 1990

Robert Charleston (Ed.): *World Ceramics,* Chartwell Books Inc., 1982

A. Faye-Halle and B. Mundt: *Nineteenth Century European Porcelain,* Trefoil Books, 1983

Frederick Litchfield: *Pottery and Porcelain, A Guide to Collectors,* 5th edition, 1951

G. Savage and H. Newman: *Illustrated Dictionary of Ceramics,* 1992

General Books (Continental)

Geoffrey Godden: *Godden's Guide to European Porcelain,* Barrie & Jenkins, 1993

Reginald Haggar: *Encyclopaedia of Continental Pottery and Porcelain,* 1960

William Honey: *German Porcelain,* Faber & Faber, 1947

William Honey: *French Porcelain,* Faber & Faber, 1950

Arthur Lane: *Italian Porcelain,* Faber & Faber, 1964

E. Pauls-Eisenbeiss: *German Porcelain of the Eighteenth Century,* Barrie & Jenkins, 1972

General Books (English)

Michael Berthoud: *A Compendium of British Cups,* Micawber, 1990

Peter Bradshaw: *Eighteenth Century English Porcelain Figures,* Antique Collectors' Club, 1981

John and Margaret Cushion: *A Collector's History of British Porcelain,* Antique Collectors' Club, 1992

Geoffrey Godden: *British Porcelain, an Illustrated Guide,* Barrie & Jenkins, 1990 reprint

Geoffrey Godden: *Encyclopaedia of British Porcelain Manufacturers,* Barrie & Jenkins, 1988

Geoffrey Godden (Ed.): *Staffordshire Porcelain,* Granada, 1983

William Honey: *Old English Porcelain* (Ed. F. Barrett), Faber & Faber, 1977

Philip Miller and Michael Berthoud: *An Anthology of British Teapots,* Micawber, 1985

Henry Sandon: *British Pottery and Porcelain,* John Gifford, 1980

John Sandon: *The Phillips Guide to English Porcelain,* Merehurst, 1989

Bernard Watney: *English Blue and White Porcelain,* Faber & Faber, 1973

Oriental Porcelain

Harry Garner: *Oriental Blue and White,* 1970

Geoffrey Godden: *Oriental Export Market Porcelain,* Granada, 1979

David Howard: *Chinese Armorial Porcelain,* Faber & Faber, 1974

David Howard and John Ayres: *China for the West,* 1978

Duncan Macintosh: *Chinese Blue and White Porcelain,* Antique Collectors' Club, 1986/1994

Margaret Medley: *The Chinese Potter,* Oxford, 1976

Oriental Ceramic Society: *Porcelain For Palaces,* British Museum, 1990

David Howard, *A Tale of Three Cities, Canton, Shanghai & Hong Kong,* Sotheby's, 1997

American Porcelain

Edwin Atlee Barber: *The Pottery and Porcelain of the United States,* 1976

Alice Cooney Frelinghuysen: *American Porcelain,* Abrams, 1989

Index

Page numbers in bold refer to illustrations